ROUTLEDGE LIBRARY EDITIONS:
TRADE UNIONS

Volume 6

I0095016

TRADE UNIONS AND POLITICS IN THE 1980S

TRADE UNIONS AND POLITICS IN THE 1980S

The 1984 Act and Political Funds

DEREK FATCHETT

R Routledge
Taylor & Francis Group

LONDON AND NEW YORK

First published in 1987 by Croom Helm Ltd.

This edition first published in 2023
by Routledge
4 Park Square, Milton Park, Abingdon, Oxon OX14 4RN

and by Routledge
605 Third Avenue, New York, NY 10158

Routledge is an imprint of the Taylor & Francis Group, an informa business

© 1987 Derek Fatchett

British Library Cataloguing in Publication Data
A catalogue record for this book is available from the British Library

ISBN: 978-1-032-37553-3 (Set)
ISBN: 978-1-032-37820-6 (Volume 6) (hbk)
ISBN: 978-1-032-37839-8 (Volume 6) (pbk)
ISBN: 978-1-003-34218-2 (Volume 6) (ebk)

DOI: 10.4324/9781003342182

Publisher's Note
The publisher has gone to great lengths to ensure the quality of this reprint but points out that some imperfections in the original copies may be apparent.

Disclaimer
The publisher has made every effort to trace copyright holders and would welcome correspondence from those they have been unable to trace.

TRADE UNIONS AND POLITICS IN THE 1980s

The 1984 Act and Political Funds

DEREK FATCHETT

CROOM HELM
London • New York • Sydney

© 1987 Derek Fatchett
Croom Helm Ltd, Provident House, Burrell Row,
Beckenham, Kent, BR3 1AT
Croom Helm Australia, 44-50 Waterloo Road,
North Ryde, 2113, New South Wales

British Library Cataloguing in Publication Data

Fatchett, Derek
    Trade unions and politics in the 1980s:
    the 1984 act and political funds.
    1. Trade-unions — Great Britain —
    Political activity. 2. Great Britain —
    Politics and government — 1964-
    I. Title
    322'.2'0941   HD6667
    ISBN 0-7099-4903-0

Published in the USA by
Croom Helm
in association with Methuen, Inc.
29 West 35th Street
New York, NY 10001

Library of Congress Cataloging-in-Publication Data

Printed and bound in Great Britain by Mackays of Chatham Ltd, Kent

CONTENTS

INTRODUCTION

Writing in the mid-1970s, Clarke [1] claimed that 'the trade unions remain the most maligned organisations in society. If the mass media are to be believed, then trade unions are responsible single-handedly for the disruption of industry, the decline of the economy, and the undermining of the social rights and privileges that traditionally have held together the delicate fabric of society. Implicit in such lurid descriptions is the belief that the trade union movement has attained a position of unassailable power which threatens the foundation of democracy; governments, it is sometimes even asserted, are mere playthings in the hands of the big battalions of the unions.' The perceptions which Clarke discussed can be analysed at two levels: firstly, against certain objective criteria, to determine whether they may be true; and, secondly, in relation to the ability of those perceptions to shape and to mould a broader agenda.

Measuring the validity of any set of perceptions, especially in such a contentious area as trade unionism, is bound to inspire further controversy. Nevertheless, certain characteristics of trade unionism in general, and British trade unionism, in particular, can be stated. For the unions, the exercise of power is intrinsically overt and negative: overt because power depends upon the actual or threatened use of industrial sanctions, all of which are largely visible and obvious; negative because, in the nature of a society where access to power is related to the control of capital, trade unions will, by definition, be reactive organisations, responding to change either proposed by the immediate employers, or taking place in the wider society.

The 1960s, and even more, the 1970s, had drawn, for a variety of reasons, attention to the negative power of unions. Collective bargaining, free from government intervention, had always been seen as the principal means of furthering the interests of trade union members. In addition, that means had been elevated in status to a cherished goal in its own right; from that, certain implications flow for the role of trade unions in politics, and their relationship with government, of whichever political description.

The relationship between government and unions was brought into sharp focus by the declining performance of the British economy, and by that prescription which regarded the control of wages as the key to halting decline. There were two policy responses to this prescription: firstly, there were those attempts either to regulate wages, or to reorganise the institutions of industrial relations; and secondly, there were those initiatives which sought to find agreement between government and the trade unions either just on the appropriate level of wage increase, or on wages, and other slightly broader issues. In turn, however, in their different ways, both these responses could be seen as threatening the right of trade unions to bargain freely with employers; in defending that right, and in reacting to a political agenda determined by others, trade unions could be interpreted as threatening the ability of governments to govern.

It is, at this point, that analysis and perception interact. Analysis might uphold the view that trade union power is largely reactive and abstentive; perceptions, on the other hand, may lead many to a different conclusion, which emphasises the alleged unaccountable and damaging nature of trade unionism. In this way, the controversy surrounding the character and the extent of power exerted by trade unions became a subject of acute political controversy. In 1974, the Conservative Government sought re-election on the basis that they needed a renewed mandate in order to combat trade union power; the slogan, 'Who governs Britain?' became central to that 1974 election. And, then, in 1979, the Conservatives, after the industrial disputes of the so-called 'winter of discontent', placed proposals to curb trade unions at the heart of their manifesto.

From 1979 onwards, the unions have seen whatever power they had noticeably curtailed: by the impact of record levels of unemployment, and by the Employment Acts of 1980 and 1982 which have severely circumscribed the legal scope for industrial action. And, against this challenge, the traditional responses of the trade unions bore little fruit: political marches and mobilisation occurred but were ignored by the Government, whilst industrial action was difficult to arrange as individual members were concerned about their own job security, and often faced an employer prepared to take advantage of the harsh realities of the new economic climate.

At the time of the Heath Government in the early 1970s, Coates and Topham (1972, p. 15) concluded that 'the Labour Movement, like all other institutions of contemporary society, is in the midst of a great crisis in which a moody flux of ideas and actions stirs, seethes, and at times bubbles over'. If some would doubt whether crisis was an appropriate term for the state of the unions in the early 1970s, there would be few who would not endorse such a conclusion in the early 1980s, especially after the general election of 1983, which gave the Conservatives the opportunity to pursue further measures against the unions. And, at the time, the compensating moody flux of ideas and actions, to which Coates and Topham referred a decade earlier, was strikingly absent. Confusion, born out of depression and despair, more clearly corresponded to the state of the unions.

It was against this background, with the unions apparently bereft of new ideas and responses that the Government, through the 1984 Trade Union Act, imposed the requirement that unions should, by ballot, seek the support of their members, if they were to continue holding a political fund, and hence, play a political role. As we shall discuss in greater detail later, this new requirement appeared, at the time, to present the trade unions with, if not an insurmountable obstacle, at least with one which was likely to prove particularly hazardous.

This book, after tracing the historical and sociological dimensions in Chapters 1-3, will analyse in Chapter 4, with the benefit of certain new questionnaire material, the nature of the trade unions' involvement in the Labour Party. Chapters 5-7 provide the opportunity of discussing in detail the review campaigns, and their implications, both for trade unions specifically, and for politics in general. From the viewpoint of the trade unions, this book tells of an experience which has, for the Thatcher era, been uniquely successful and innervating, opening up new approaches to campaigning. It is a story which scarcely seemed possible when the first review ballot was held in April 1985.

Finally, I would like to thank all those who have made this book a reality: my former colleagues, Keith Forrester and Bruce Spencer for their comments on the initial draft; Sue Vasey, Andrew James, Maggie Boyle and Zoe Smith who assisted me significantly in the collection of material, and in the preparation of the initial draft; Judy Box, who strove hard and successfully to turn my handwriting into a neat and final typescript; and, my wife Anita, and sons, Gareth and Brendan who assisted in many, often unnoticed and unthanked, ways. Thanks to all of them, this book is the result of a co-operative venture, as most works of this type must and should be. The final responsibility is, however, mine, as are the opinions and conclusions. The writing, however, has been a pleasure as it tells of events which might lead to the reshaping of British trade unionism.

NOTES

1. Tom Clarke, 'The Raison D'Etre of Trade Unionism' in Tom Clarke and Laurie Clements (1977), p. 7.

Chapter One

TRADE UNION POLITICAL FUNDS -
AN HISTORICAL PERSPECTIVE

To understand the current rules, which determine the manner
in which trade unions organise and manage their political
funds, it is necessary to appreciate the historical dimension.
Much of the debate, and all the constraints which characterised the 1985/6 review ballot campaigns, can be traced to
earlier parliamentary and political conflicts. This chapter will
analyse those conflicts, and particularly note the extent to
which earlier arguments have helped to shape the current
agenda.

PRE-1913

In his work on trade union structure and organisation,
Turner (1962) hypothesised two ideal typical models of trade
unions: open and closed. As a heuristic device, that approach
may help towards an understanding of the political role of
trade unions, and their involvement in funding their own
political party.
     For Turner, the closed unions would be concentrated in
particular, specified industries, often themselves limited in
their locations. Of special interest, in this context, are the
methods adopted to further the aims of union members. These
aims would be enhanced by the effective enforcement of a
pre-entry closed shop; recruitment to the trade, therefore,
would be limited and strictly controlled, with the objective of
ensuring that employers had no alternative but to recruit
labour from amongst those approved by the union.
     Certain characteristics flowed from this approach: firstly,
internal union discipline and solidarity became so important
that they assumed the role not just of a means to an end, but
an end in themselves; secondly, this internal solidarity and
discipline helped to develop a craft or occupational
consciousness, rather than a class consciousness, as one's
own position in the labour market depended to a great extent
upon excluding other workers and their interests; and

4

thirdly, because of the local nature of organisation, and the preoccupation with the labour market, politics, in a more general sense, appeared to be of secondary importance, if not totally irrelevant. Notions of overthrowing capitalism seemed out of context against this background, when advantages could be seen to arise from the very market system which so defined capitalism. In historical terms, the golden era for what in practice can be regarded as a close approximation to closed unions, came in the mid-decades of the nineteenth century with craft unions, such as the Amalgamated Society of Engineers. For those unions, the emphasis was upon peaceful collaboration and conciliation with the employers; the search for respectability, and with it an inevitable degree of conservatism, was paramount.

In Turner's contrasting model, open-ness was both a defining and limiting characteristic. Open unions could not be selective in their recruitment; they would initially take any member in any industry. Numbers, rather than selectivity, became the name of the game, with a post-entry closed shop offering the only option of imposing any degree of control upon employers. The constraints upon collective bargaining power are readily apparent; strength could exist only in those conditions where there was a general shortage of labour. Rising levels of unemployment would not simply sap bargaining strength, but they would equally challenge the very core of the unions' organisation. Against these intrinsic weaknesses, collective bargaining did not necessarily offer such an attractive means of advancing members interests; an additional alternative might need to be explored. And, it was in political campaigning that an alternative was to be found.

In practice, open unions can be traced back to the surge of new unionism amongst semi-skilled and unskilled workers in the last two decades of the nineteenth century. It was these new general unions which gave trade union political involvement a much higher profile. For them, politics could not be regarded as a luxury, but as a necessary condition for their survival and growth.

It can be argued that the requirements of the open unions for political action, combined with the intrinsic conservatism of the closed unions, helped to shape the nature of political involvement. The open unions demanded political action; the closed unions defined the approach in a way which led to what has been termed labourism: that is, that body of working class political 'theory and practice which accepted the possibility of social change within the existing framework of society, which rejected revolutionary violence and action implicit in Chartist ideas of physical force: and which increasingly recognised the working of political democracy of the parliamentary variety as the practical means of achieving its own aims and objectives' (Coates 1975, p. 6).

A further reinforcement of the parliamentary approach can be found in the employing classes, own commitment to the notion of parliamentary democracy. As Allen (1966, pp. 31 & 32) has noted in the more general context of trade unionism, 'a government which is a consequence of a parliamentary democratic system and which professes a belief in that system cannot readily legislate away the freedom of association of which the existence of trade unions is an expression'. That argument equally applies to trade unions in their efforts to secure a political role, especially when the early involvement was largely parliamentarian in nature, and centred upon the existing two party political system.

As the male franchise was extended in the second half of the nineteenth century, unions tried to achieve their political objectives through support for sympathetic candidates from both the Liberal and Conservative Parties, although, as one would expect, with an obvious bias towards the Liberals. However, in the last two decades of the century, coinciding with the growth of the general unions, a broad dissatisfaction emerged with this search for sympathetic MPs and the argument for a distinct party of labour gained ground. Efforts were made to secure the election of working class men to Parliament, and in 1886, for instance, the TUC established a Labour Electoral Committee, with that specific objective, although even at this stage, loyalties and affiliation were still strongly tied to the Liberal Party.

The emerging pattern of trade union support for candidates of working class origin, who were seen as either Liberal supporters, or independent Labour, was evident in the 1892 General Election. Trade Unions assisted financially 28 Liberal candidates (The Lib-Labs) of whom 12 were successful; and 17 independent Labour candidates of whom 3 were successful; Keir Hardie, John Burns and J.H. Wilson. This division between Liberal and Labour sympathies came to dominate the labour movement's debate about parliamentary representations in the 1890s. For instance, in 1893, a fund was established by the TUC to support working class candidates, but within a year only two unions had affiliated. Similarly, in 1896, Liberal sympathies were still sufficiently strong for a resolution to establish a political fund to be defeated at the TUC.

Alongside these continuing expressions of support for the Liberal Party must be seen the establishment in 1893 of the Independent Labour Party. Although the ILP sought to maintain its own independence in decision making, and in the process largely disqualified itself from trade union financial resources, the pressure for a grand alliance of trade unions, and individual socialists grew, leading in 1900 to the formation of the Labour Representation Committee. Even at that stage, doubts were expressed by leading trade unionists about this more open political role, and, in particular, about the willingness of trade unionists to contribute financially:

Will Thorne of the Gasworkers Union admitted that, whilst there was no difficulty in getting money from individual socialists, because they had a definite object before them, and they knew what they were paying for, when it came to trade unionists, it was another matter [1]. Contributions to the Labour Representation Committee were initially slow in coming, but much of that, and the related political orientation, was radically changed by the Taff Vale Railway Co. case of 1901 [2], as a result of which trade unions, as institutions, were exposed to substantial new areas of tortious liability.

Referring back to the earlier quote from Allen (1966) in which he argued that the state would recognise the freedom of association, it might be necessary to couch that tolerance in a limited context; freedom of association was quite acceptable until the power of trade unions threatened employers' prerogatives. To a significant degree, the more open and aggressive style of the new unions in the 1890s could be perceived by the employers as such a threat.

The judiciary in the Taff Vale Railway Co. case acted as the instrument for challenging trade union power, as, by their judgement, they were able to indicate how exposed trade unions were to legal action. The reaction to that judgement is of importance. Firstly, Parliament, aware of the pressure of organised labour, granted, not rights to act in certain ways, but immunities from common law action, if certain acts were performed in the context of an industrial dispute. The 1906 Trades Dispute Act, whilst providing a framework of labour law which lasted for more than half a century, also placed trade unions at the edge of legality, and on the defensive. The unions were on the defensive because, in contrast to other liberal capitalist countries, they were not granted rights; and because immunities would always prove to be subject to possible redefinition and restriction through judicial interpretation. Commenting on the 1974 and 1976 Trade Union and Labour Relations Act, for instance, Simpson drew attention to how the provision of those Acts had to be stronger and clearer than the 1906 Act, in order to overcome the impact of judicial intervention during the 1960s.

Secondly, the Taff Vale judgement, ironically, stimulated the pressures for a greater political role for trade unions, partially shifting the balance from industrial to political action, and preparing the ground for the 1906 formation of the Labour Party, which occurred with scarcely any dissent in the trade union movement. This new party of labour represented both a threat to the two main existing parties, but, also with its potentially socialist rhetoric and action, a threat to capitalism, and its employer class. The party was, of course, overwhelmingly funded by the trade unions, and it was in this financial relationship between party and unions that the judiciary was again to make a decisive intervention.

7

TRADE UNION POLITICAL FUNDS

The use of trade union funds to support the election and maintenance of Labour MPs was widely regarded as a legitimate use of trade union money, even though individual members might object to the Labour Party. This viewpoint was confirmed by a King's Bench decision in 1907: Steele v South Wales Miners Federation (1907) 1KB 361. All that changed with the judgement in Amalgamated Society of Railway Servants v Osborne (1910) AC 87.

THE OSBORNE CASE AND THE 1913 ACT

Osborne, a railway employee, objected to the use of union funds for political purposes, arguing that such a use was illegal. This contention was upheld in the House of Lords judgement, on the grounds that the statutory definition of a trade union, then to be found in the Trade Union Acts of 1871 and 1876, was exhaustive of the objects that a trade union could legally pursue. Political objects were not included in the statutory definitions, and therefore, any payment towards political objects had necessarily to be regarded as ultra vires. Unless Parliament attributed political objects to trade unions, they would be deprived of the ability to develop their political action, which was now characterised mainly but not wholly in the formation of the Labour Party.

The Osborne Judgement seemed, however, to run counter to majority legal opinion, a conclusion apparently supported by the Attorney General, Sir Rufus Isaacs, when he introduced the Second Reading of the 1913 Trade Union Act:

> The judgement pronounced by the highest judicial tribunal of the land, made it clear for the first time that a trade union could not devote its funds or could not make levies for political purposes. Up to that time, undoubtedly, the view has been held by the vast majority of lawyers in this country that trade unions could use their funds for political purposes, and there was even a decision in the Courts to that effect [3].

Whatever the legal merits of the Osborne case, there can be little doubt about the problems it caused to the trade unions. Political activity would henceforth be heavily circumscribed, if not totally impossible. For many trade union activists, and socialists, the Osborne case was regarded as an attempt by the employer class to strangle the new born Labour Party at birth. Liberal democracy could not allow strangulation, but the response, in the 1913 Trade Union Act, treated the trade unions in such a distinctive way that, in their political activities, they would inevitably be placed on the defensive. It may, therefore, be useful to look at the

Liberal Government's justification for the 1913 Act in some detail, as it can be argued that much of the subsequent debate about funding can be traced to that justification. Of paramount importance, the Government conceded that trade unions should be allowed a political role. 'The view we take as a Government on this matter, after very serious consideration, is that we do not think that the trade unions ought to be confined merely to the sphere of industrial activity. We think that combinations of men, of working people, joined together for the purpose of ameliorating the conditions of labour are entitled to take some part in the political life' [4].

The concession, however, was couched in terms which are integral to any understanding of trade union political funds. A distinction was introduced by this legislation between the statutory and political objects of trade unions: statutory objects being defined as the promotion of industrial interests, with the political objects being regarded as no more than the promotion of party and candidates, and the support of MPs. It is interesting to note that the Attorney-General claimed to find it difficult to differentiate on every occasion between political and industrial activities: 'I found it quite impossible by any definition to draw the line between what is industrial and what is political' [5]. Nevertheless, a distinction was drawn in Section 3 of the Act, along the lines already referred to.

Having made the distinction, the Government then proceeded to establish two further conditions. Firstly, political activity, as defined in the Act, could only be financed from a separate political fund; and to establish that fund, the unions would be forced to ballot their members. Secondly, unlike the general membership contribution, individual trade unionists would be allowed to opt out of paying to the political fund. The justification for this right to opt out - a right which was further enshrined by the provision that no member who opted out should be disadvantaged in any way - was based on the argument that no member should be expected to contribute towards political objects with which he may not agree. No such argument was considered in relation to the general industrial contribution.

The result of the Liberal Government's approach can be seen as long-lasting; instead of fusing the industrial and the political, a rigid line was drawn between them, with the political being treated in a radically different manner. This distinction can be interpreted not simply as strengthening the viewpoint that primacy should be accorded to industrial activity, but helped to convey an impression, which has lived with the trade unions subsequently, that political activity was somehow less legitimate. Here are sown some of the seeds of trade union defensiveness in relation to their political role.

It is often stated that the 1913 Act helped to establish a broad consensus for political funding. That conclusion is not, in any way, consistent with the behaviour of the Conservatives during the debates on the 1913 Act, and, intermittently, in subsequent years. As we shall see at a later stage, the arguments used by the Conservatives in 1913 were repeated with equal conviction in 1983. The main objections by the Conservatives in 1913 were twofold: firstly, if people wanted to contribute to a political party, they could do so, but the mechanism of a political fund, with the right to opt out, would ensure, either through intimidation or through deliberate creation of bureaucratic difficulties, that many trade unionists would be paying to a political party which they did not support. The Conservative spokesman, Slater, summed up that argument in these words: 'You are going to take the money of men who are convinced Liberals or Conservatives, and you are going to apply that money beyond a doubt to socialistic purpose' [6]. These words could easily have been used in 1983 by Tebbit in his role as Secretary of State for Employment in a Conservative Government.

Secondly, the Conservatives also argued that the definition of industrial was much too wide: for them, many activities which the Government was prepared to consider industrial, should be considered as political. A new definition of political was required, so as to embrace these activities, again a viewpoint repeated in the 1983 debates.

As might be expected, the Labour Party's attitude to the 1913 Act was generally hostile. As the main spokesman for the Party, Clynes employed a number of arguments which have an equally modern relevance. Firstly, though, he cited legal opinion to cast further doubt upon the Osborne judgement. 'From 1871 down to 1908 the trade unions, without any interference and without any alleged illegality have been quite able to spend their money by their votes of majorities for the purpose of sending their men here (Parliament). Conservative working men and Socialist working men have been contributing towards the support of Liberal working men who have sat on these benches' [7]. Clynes' main demand was for a simple restoration of what was regarded by the overwhelming majority of legal opinion as the correct interpretation of the law prior to the Osborne case.

As for the arguments which have run through the decades, Clynes makes two points. There is, firstly an antipathy towards the political/industrial division of trade union activities, a division, of course, which formed the basis of the 1913 Act. The pursuit of working class interests in the struggle against capital did not lend itself to easy categorisation; class conflict was all embracing. Secondly, the ability to opt out of the implications of a majority decision was considered as anathema to the values and practice of trade union decision making. The whole structure of collective democracy in the trade unions depends upon the minority accepting the majority decision, whilst, at the same time, enjoying the right to reverse that decision at some later stage. The ability to opt out of the political levy payment transposed the very principles of collective decision making; not only that, but in this new category of trade union activity - the political - the individual member was offered two bites of the cherry: the first in the necessary ballot on whether the union should have a political fund, and the second in the right to opt out of contributing to that fund, if a majority voted affirmatively.

For the Labour MPs the defence of trade union practice and principles alone made the Bill unwelcome. Alongside these important, but particular, criticisms, there was a strong feeling that the real, but unstated intention of the 1913 Act was to forestall the development of the emergent Labour Party. This fear was summed up by Clynes: 'We are now engaged ... in this effort to legally obstruct the entry into this House of the trade union representatives who are in it already' [8].

These deeper anxieties about the Act resulting in the collapse of funding for the new Labour Party did not materialise. As was to be repeated some seventy years later, the ballots, required under the Act, produced solid support for the approval of trade union political funds. The outcome of voting under the 1913 Act was 605,437 (62.5%) for and 363,222 (37.5%) against, a two to one victory; but the majority in some unions was quite narrow. The Amalgamated Society of Carpenters and Joiners voted 13,336-11,738 in favour, while the Miners Federation of Great Britain only voted yes by 261,643-195,800 (Leopold, 1986).

1913-47

The 1913 Act has often been seen as providing a consensual basis for the funding of the Labour Party. Looked at from the perspective and the experience of the years which immediately followed the passing of the 1913 Act, no such cosy consensus appeared to exist. In the debate on the 1927 Trades Dispute Act, Clynes from the Labour benches emphasised the substantial efforts of the Conservative Party to undermine the 1913 Act:

'This Bill is not due to the fact that there was anything like a general strike last year. The industrial troubles of 1926 are not the cause, though they are being made the occasion for this particular purpose. Eleven separate Bills have been introduced from that side of the House (i.e. the Conservatives) during the last six or seven years, all exhibiting the spirit of this Bill, and aiming at the present liberties and activities of organised labour' [9]. In fact, Clynes went further: he also drew attention to the extra-parliamentary activities of the Conservative Party.

11

Millions of Tory leaflets ... have been circulated to Tory organisations and thousands of speeches have been made from Tory platforms ... I particularly ask the attention of the Prime Minister to the fact that for a long time now it has been the purpose of his considerable following to sow internal dissention in the trade unions as between their members and their leaders, to exhibit the trade unions as wasteful, money-squandering organisations. [10].

The central theme of both the intra- and extra-parliamentary campaigns centred upon the ability to opt out of the political levy. For many Conservatives, the opting-out principle could be criticised on two grounds: firstly, that in principle, legislation which required individuals to express their political opposition to a collective decision was, by definition, an infringement upon individual liberty. And, secondly, in the exercise of that individual liberty, intimidation of those individuals wishing to opt out would be both possible, and, in practice, widespread. According to one Conservative, in the debate on a Private Member's Bill introduced in 1925, the principle of opting-in would 'limit the opportunities of coercion' [11].

The opportunity for the change to the 1913 Act was provided by the 1926 General Strike. Hitherto, even in 1925, the Conservatives in office had been reluctant to introduce any change which might potentially upset the delicate balance which existed in industry between capital and labour. This concern is evident in Baldwin's contribution to the debate on the 1925 Private Member's Bill. As Prime Minister, whilst supporting the principles of political liberty enunciated in the Bill, Baldwin talked much more in terms of the future of British industry being secured by reconciliation and partnership between the two sides: he looked for people on both sides of industry 'to steer their respective ships side by side, instead of making for head-on collision' [12].

That spirit of reconciliation did not survive the 1926 General Strike. The power of capital was now in the ascendancy and obviously so. Trade unions, and their political parties, were to experience a difficult period. At the workplace, the ability to bargain, and to organise was substantially reduced, with active trade unionists in the front line for dismissal. As the trade unions lost their industrial muscle, so the basis of the funding of their political party was subjected to attack. Certainly this was the dominant view, in the labour movement, of the 1927 Trades Dispute Act: an Act which declared sympathetic, general strikes to be illegal; which banned trade union membership for civil servants in relation to TUC affiliates; and which, much to the pleasure of many sections of the Conservative Party, enacted opting-in, rather than opting-out for payment of the political levy. In her diaries Beatrice Webb (1956, pp. 138-9) saw the Act as 'the governing class reprisal for the General Strike and the miners refusal to accept the employers terms ... If the Bill had dealt solely with the general and national strike, as attempts to coerce the rest of the community, there would have been some sense in it ... But the clause against the political levy shows a class madness and meanness in a virulent form. A levy is the only way in which a working class party can raise funds, and it is certainly more ethically fastidious than the "sale of honours" or subsidies from the great financial interests.'

Interestingly, Webb (1956, pp. 140-1) regarded the Parliamentary debate concerned with the Act as depressing: 'There is unreality in the Parliamentary debate. The Tories are determined to make hay of trade unions while the sun of their majority shines; the Labour Party is equally determined to use the Trade Union Bill as an election bogey - there is no interchange of thought and no desire to compromise or join the largest measure of consent. Each party appeals to its own mob. The Liberals have been submerged by the tempest.' Whilst this comment adequately illustrates Beatrice Webb's dislike of certain aspects of party politics, it equally highlights the real divide which then existed on the question of funding the Labour Party.

In relation to political funds, the most significant change contained in the 1927 Act was the introduction of opting-in, rather than opting-out of the political levy. The Conservative Party's wish for this change was at last realised. In addition to the more general principle of individual freedom, an argument based upon intimidation was employed by the Conservative Government to justify the change. An equation, maybe tempting but probably false, between those who voted against the political fund in the initial ballots, and those who opted out of the political levy, was drawn. It was argued that, because there was a difference between the numbers of members who voted against the establishment of a political fund, and those who opted out of paying the levy, there was intrinsic evidence of intimidation. For instance, a Conservative member made that case in the following terms during the second reading debate on the 1927 Act: 'Some 600,000 took advantage of the secret ballot, but when it came to signing a form of open dissent from the trade union leaders then there were only 100,000. There is not the slightest doubt ... that every sort of obstacle has been put in the way' [13].

Indeed, turning that argument on its head, the Attorney-General, Sir Douglas Hogg, suggested that, if unions were not practising or involved in intimidation, they had no reason to fear the change to opting-in. 'Such Trade Unions as legally observe the provisions of the Act of 1913 will find that the enactment of Clause 4 (the opting-in clause) will make practically no difference. On the other hand, those who use methods of intimidation, or raise difficulties against their members will no doubt be affected, and may be seriously affected' [14]. It is difficult to comment extensively upon the allegation of intimidation, as there is little objective evidence available either to support or to counter the assertion; although it was pointed out during the course of the debate that the Registrar of Friendly Societies had received only seven complaints during the previous year about the opting-out provision of the 1913 Act.

As one would anticipate, the 1927 Act was vigorously opposed in the House of Commons, with the normal courtesies of debate often being strained. The campaign against the Act was not, however, limited to Parliament. The National Trade Union Defence Committee, consisting of representatives of both the Labour Party and the TUC, aimed to take the campaign against the Act to every part of the country. There appears to have been some success in relation to this objective. The Labour Party's Annual Report commented that 'the work was so comprehensive in character that villages were visited which had not been touched in any previous national campaign, and which were in some cases neglected even in times of a General Election' [15]. It was claimed that 1,150 meetings and demonstrations were addressed by national speakers, with very many more local meetings with local speakers.

The climax of the campaign occurred on June 26th, 1927 when protest marches were held throughout the country to coincide with the House of Commons approving the third reading of the Bill. The Labour Party expressed a certain pride in the success of the rallies and marches: referring to the Hyde Park demonstration, it was felt that the unity of the industrial, co-operative and labour movement was such as 'to make the occasion stand out in history. The main procession, including bands, decorated co-operative vehicles, scores of trade union banners, and many thousands of marchers, was the largest which has been held in the history of the labour movement' [16].

Despite the claims in relation to the success of the campaign, the trade unions soon found themselves faced with the opting-in provision. There can be little doubt that this new regime, coupled with declining trade union membership as a result of rising unemployment, and the demoralising effect of the defeat in the 1926 General Strike, was about to inflict severe financial hardship upon the Labour Party.

The new position was soon very apparent. In the 1929 Labour Party Annual Report, the full extent of the damage could be assessed: 'At the beginning of 1926 the affiliation fees were increasing, and there was every expectation that the position would improve. Reduced trade union membership, however, led to a very substantial reduction in the Party

income, and in 1927 the passage of the Trade Disputes and
Trade Unions Act completely altered the outlook. Now that it
is possible to survey the accounts for 1928, it is evident that
the position is much worse than at any time since 1920. This
is most clearly realised by a contrast of the affiliated trade
union membership, which has fallen from 3,238,939 in 1927 to
2,025,139 in 1928' [17]. In other words, the Labour Party
had experienced a nearly 40 per cent decline in affiliated
membership. The implications of that can be seen in the
Party's finances, especially if one stresses that, coupled with
the 1927 Act, unemployment had helped reduce affiliations by
more than 50 per cent between 1920-29. Typical of the period
of the 1930s is the Party Report of 1931 which indicated a
loss of £8,500, with an expected further annual deficit of
£19,000 in 1932. The only solution, it seemed, to these
difficulties was to increase trade union affiliation fees; a move
not always welcomed by trade union leaders, particularly in
view of what they saw as the heavy burden of the political
levy on those earning low wages. Individual party membership, which increased in the 1930s from 277,000 in 1930 to
409,000 in 1939, although healthy in itself, did not provide
sufficient income to offset the loss of trade union funds.

The 1930s, then, saw the Labour Party, faced by a
reduced financial contribution from the trade unions,
enmeshed in a state of constant crisis. Finances were limited,
but the demands for political action, against a backcloth of
the collapse of the 1929-31 Government and the heavy election
defeats in 1931 and 1935, were substantial; a point which was
noted in the 1939 Report: 'The financial position of the Party
during the past ten years has been one of increasing serious-
ness. The calls upon the resources of the Party have been
pressing and, in the view of the National Executive
Committee, legitimate, and such that, in the best interests of
the movement it could not resist' [18]. Inevitably, along with
other reasons, the financial straits of the Party led to
demands for the repeal of the 1927 Act. Bevin asked for this
from the incumbent Labour Government during the 1930
Annual Conference. No action was taken in relation to Bevin's
demand; indeed, he had to wait until a Labour Government,
of which he formed a part, repealed the Act in 1946.

THE 1946 ACT AND A NEW CONSENSUS

Before looking at the detail of the 1946 legislation, it is
briefly worth pausing to comment upon the nature of Bevin's
demands. The aspirations were very limited: the aim was to
return to the provisions of the 1913 Act. Gone, it seems, was
the argument that trade union interests would be best served
by returning to the law as it was thought to stand before the
Osborne judgement. Characteristically in terms of trade union

reaction, the objective was merely defensive: to restore the previous position, and not to seek what may be regarded as an ideal solution.

The incoming Labour Government of 1945 took little time to satisfy Bevin's demands, and to repeal the 1927 Act. As far as political funds were concerned, the 1946 Trades Disputes and Trade Unions Act did no more than restore the 1913 provisions.

In introducing the Bill, the then Attorney-General, Sir Hartley Shawcross, justified the decision to reinstate the 1913 formula on the grounds that the majority decision to support a political fund placed the onus upon those, wishing not to contribute, to dissociate themselves from that majority decision. That argument was intriguingly echoed in the 1983/84 debates: as a justification for not supporting an opting-in principle, the Government in 1984 asserted that it was preferable to hold a ballot upon whether the existing membership wished to continue with the political fund. It is, however, extremely doubtful whether Government Ministers in 1984 would have shared the sentiments expressed by Shawcross in the following statement:

> The question here is very simple, whether the trade unions which by a majority have decided to have a political fund, should benefit if you like from that human inertia, as I have called it, to the extent of throwing the onus on the dissentient minority to declare their objection to contribute to particular political funds, or whether the onus should be put the other way, and whether the majority, who have already voted in favour of the political fund, should be required to go further, and fill in a form showing they wish to make a particular contribution. In any ordinary organisation like a club or company ... the minority have to toe the line [19].

Shawcross further supported his general contention by arguing that, prior to the change introduced in 1927, evidence of intimidation, forcing reluctant members to pay the levy, was difficult to find. 'The figures of the Registrar of Friendly Societies demonstrate that there is not a rag of evidence to support the view that anyone was being compelled to contribute to political funds against his will' [20]. Again, allegations of intimidation, combined with limited or no evidence to support the allegations, seem to have character-ised all the debates about political funds.

The Conservatives campaigned (both in and out of the House of Commons) around these themes, and around the supposed threats to individual liberty. Whilst Shawcross, in his speech, referred on more than one occasion, to what he perceived as the frenzied and hysterical nature of the Conservative campaign, that feeling hardly intruded into the

House of Commons debate. Eden, speaking for the Conservative Party, rarely raised what might be seen as fundamental principles. He criticised the return to opting-in, but on the grounds that if members wanted to support financially a political party, they should be prepared to take positive action to show their support. 'It is no great thing to ask that supporters of any political party should fill in a form just once' [21]. These comments were scarcely of the sort which presaged a commitment to repeal the 1946 Act: whilst Eden criticised the Bill because, for him, it did not assist in relation to the difficulties confronting the country, he did not, at any stage during his speech, say that a future Conservative Government would return to the practice of opting-in.

The changes introduced by the 1946 Act both benefited Labour, and provided the accepted basis of funding for more than three decades. The benefit is instantly recognisable, with Labour being able to take advantage of what Shawcross has described as human inertia. In 1945 2.9m trade unionists paid the political levy; in 1947 on a 10 per cent increase in trade union membership, the number of levy payers had almost doubled to 5.6 million.

THE POST 1946 CONSENSUS

Apart from immediately benefiting the Labour Party financially, the 1946 Act's more important contribution was to be found in its success in taking trade union political funds out of controversy. Maybe this lack of controversy can be related to the more general political consensus which emerged, and which itself can be seen as surviving through to the mid-1970s. It was a consensus in which the Labour movement was broadly prepared to accept the need for a mixed economy, and with it, the requirement of profit as the criterion of success and value. For their part, the Conservatives and the employers committed themselves to the aim of full employment, and to the continuation of, and possible improvement of, the facilities of the welfare state which had been established by the 1945 Labour Government. For some, such as Saville (1957/8) the welfare state provided no more than 'a reasonable degree of economic efficiency by the erection of social and political shock absorbers, whose function is to offset the gross inequalities and the natural insecurities of the capitalist order'; for the majority of the labour movement, however, the welfare state and full employment were regarded as such significant gains that the terms of the implied political consensus were considered neither unacceptable nor burdensome.

Against this framework, in which the broad organising principles for society were widely accepted, it is scarcely surprising that political funding failed to find a place on the agenda: trade union funding for the Labour Party, and company support for the Conservatives, could even be seen as part of the institutional arrangements which underpinned the broader consensus.

The Donovan Commission (1965-1968), which was established at a time when industrial relations in general, and unofficial strikes in particular, were attracting more attention, consistent with this consensus on funding, devoted little attention to the question of trade union finance for the Labour Party.

According to the Commission's final report (1968), a few representations were received in favour of opting-in; in addition, a small number of references were made to the alleged difficulties in opting-out. Amongst those expressing the view that intimidation existed was Robert Carr, the Conservative Spokesman on Employment. The Commission asked Mr. Carr 'whether he had specific instances in mind, and if so, whether he would be prepared to supply details, if necessary in confidence'. According to the Commission, in a courteous reply, Carr made it clear 'that he was not basing his remarks on detailed examples but was speaking in general terms. He thought, however, that he might be able to supply details of specific cases if given the time - an expectation apparently not fulfilled' (1968, Para 923). Given that this small flame of possible controversy was soon extinguished, it clearly came as no surprise when the Commission recommended no change in the present rules for political funding.

SUMMARY

This chapter has been concerned with, firstly, the processes by which the trade unions came to see the need for a political role; and, secondly, with the extent to which the development of that role was constrained by judicial intervention, and the legislative reaction to that intervention. Despite the subsequent changes which were enacted, and then repealed, as a result of the 1927 and 1946 Acts, the characteristics of the 1913 Act have shaped a great deal of the later debate.

The 1913 Act succeeded in particularising and marginalising the trade unions' political role. It was a marginalisation which the unions totally opposed, but later, maybe through necessity, came, first to acquiesce in, and, later, to accept. It was, however, a marginalisation which induced a defensiveness about the unions' political role, often leading to neglect. And it was that neglect which created the opportunity for the 1984 Act.

NOTES

1. TUC Conference Report, 1900, pp. 159-60.
2. Taff Vale Railway Co. v Amalgamated Society of Railway Servants (1910) AC 426.
3. Hansard 6th August, 1912, Col. 2976.
4. Col. 2977.
5. Col. 2980.
6. Col. 2992.
7. Col. 3012.
8. Col. 3010.
9. Hansard 2nd May, 1927, Col. 1340.
10. Col. 1340
11. Hansard 6th March, 1925, Col. 832.
12. Col. 839.
13. Hansard 2nd May, 1927, Col. 1495.
14. Col. 1326.
15. Labour Party Annual Report, 1927, p. 31.
16. P. 32.
17. Labour Party Annual Report, 1929, p. 220.
18. Labour Party Annual Report, 1939, p. 76.
19. Hansard 12th February, 1946, Col. 209.
20. Col. 209.
21. Col. 224.

Chapter Two

THE 1984 ACT: ITS BACKGROUND AND IMPLICATIONS

In the previous chapter, we have analysed the development of trade union political funds, and, in particular, the statutory framework in which they function. This chapter will look at the extent to which the 1984 Act re-drew that framework, and also, by way of introduction, at the relationship between the 1984 Act and the other industrial relations legislation which the Government had already introduced.

BACKGROUND TO 1984 ACT

The first two decades of the post-war era were characterised not just by a substantial degree of political consensus, but by economic growth and annual increases in real living standards. It was with the weakening of the economy in the 1970s that there emerged a new keenness for alternative political and economic theories and strategies. It was, at this point, that influential sections of the Conservative Party, including the party leader, Margaret Thatcher, and those close to her, became committed to a set of political ideas usually described as monetarism [1].

To be effective, in practice, on its own terms, monetarism would need to achieve, amongst other things, a marked reduction in the power of organised labour. For monetarists, post-war Keynesian economic management had stimulated the power of labour in two distinct and regrettable ways: firstly, by generating conditions in which the demands for labour often in the post-1945 period, outstripped the supply of labour, thereby reducing the power of the employer at the point of production; and secondly, by increasing the provision of state welfare payments and facilities, which could be regarded in theory, if not always in practice, as both redistributive, and as lessening the rigours of the labour market.

To turn the wish to reduce trade union power into a political possibility, it was necessary to focus attention upon the alleged abuses of that power. This was achieved with some effectiveness, by making constant references to the propensity to take industrial action, and to the perception that unions were led by 'militants'. The ground for this type of political argument was especially fertile, given the widely held view that it was trade union power which had led to the defeat of the Wilson Government in 1970, and of the Heath Government in 1974. Typical of the comments made by leading Conservative spokesmen were those made by Sir Geoffrey Howe, in 1978, who was at that stage the Shadow Chancellor of the Exchequer. 'Union members increasingly contract out of Labour Party membership. A mixed Labour and Communist Union hierarchy claims to speak for a membership of whom virtually none vote Communist - barely even vote Labour any longer. Yet the questionable reality remains in the form of a union leadership pledged to maintain a failed but compliant Labour Government in power' [2].

It came, therefore, as no surprise that the Conservative manifesto for the 1979 General Election committed an incoming Government to a programme of what was called trade union reform. The Conservatives accused the Labour Government of 1974-9 of enacting a 'militants' charter', which, in their opinion, 'tilted the balance of power in bargaining throughout industry away from responsible management and towards unions, and sometimes towards unofficial groups of workers acting in defiance of their official union leadership' [3]. Three areas of reform were advocated: picketing, the closed shop, and the need for wider participation. There was no direct reference to trade union political funds, although it was stated that 'wider use of secret ballots for decision-making throughout the trade union movement should be given every encouragement' [4]. Perhaps this provided the subsequent justification for the review ballots.

The incoming 1979 Government differed from its Conservative predecessor of 1970-4 in its approach to industrial relations in one important respect. The earlier Heath Government had opted for one all embracing piece of legislation: the 1971 Industrial Relations Act. There was to be no repeat of that approach: this time a step by step method was preferred.

At the time of writing, there have been three separate major pieces of industrial relations legislation: the 1980 and 1982 Employment Acts, and the 1984 Trade Union Act. The 1980 and 1982 legislation aimed at a number of different aspects of trade union activities. Firstly, there were restrictions on those aspects of internal organisation which were designed to strengthen union bargaining power in relation to an employer; the ability to maintain a pre-entry or post-entry closed shop was severely curtailed. Secondly, the possibility of organising secondary or sympathetic boycotts in support of industrial action was so heavily constrained that it

has become almost impossible to pursue legally the sort of
action which had for so long characterised much industrial
conflict. And, thirdly, the law was so changed as to put
trade union funds at risk from actions at tort, a fundamental
reversal of one of the underpinning principles of the 1906
Trade Disputes Act.

The 1984 Trade Union Act made further inroads into the
practices adopted by trade unions in relation to industrial
disputes: in order to enjoy the admittedly less valuable
immunities for actions committed during the course of an
industrial dispute, unions would now require a majority vote
in a strike ballot. It was, however, in the two other main
elements of the 1984 Act that the Government's proposals
broke new ground and caused so much controversy. Firstly,
elections to a union's principal executive committee would, by
law, be required to be held in accordance with the guidelines
set out in the Act. Internal aspects of trade union democracy
were no longer to be left to the members' own wishes, and to
the traditional processes of change within the unions; the
Government was effectively involving itself in the internal
administration of a voluntary body.

And, of course, secondly, there was the proposal to
subject trade union political funds to periodic ballots. As one
would anticipate, the reaction of trade union leaders and
Labour Party representatives was immediately to label this as
a party political attack upon the funds of the Labour Party.
John Smith, the Labour Party's employment spokesman,
summed it up in the following way, which for him left no
possible area of misunderstanding about motives. 'This is the
plainly and avowedly party political part of the Bill. Its main
provisions attempt to do harm to the funds of the Labour
Party, and thereby advantage the Conservative Party and any
other parties in the state apart from the Labour Party. That
is the simple objective of this part of the Bill' [5].

THE GOVERNMENT'S CASE FOR THE 1984 ACT

Whether Smith was correct in attributing to the Government
the intention of damaging the Labour Party will remain a
matter for party political debate, and conjecture; what is true
is that the Government could not present its case to the
public in those terms. In all the discussions on the 1983
Green Paper, and subsequent proposals and legislation, the
Government defined their position in relation to two themes:
firstly, the lapse of time since the initial, and in most cases
only ballot, and secondly, the discrepancy between the percentage of union members paying the political levy, and those
supporting the Labour Party.

The Time Gap

As was pointed out in Chapter 1, most political fund ballots took place in the immediate years subsequent to the enactment of the 1913 Act. Hardly any trade unionists, who were existing members in 1984, had participated in a ballot on this issue. For the Government, despite the right which was enshrined in the 1913 Act for individuals to opt out of paying the levy, the lack of a ballot for approximately a 70 year period was sufficient justification in itself for a new ballot. In introducing to the House of Commons a statement on trade unions in July 1983, the then Secretary of State, Norman Tebbit put the argument in these terms:

> The present members of trade unions should not be bound for ever by a ballot that may well have been taken before any of them were born [6].

A similar theme was reinforced by the then Parliamentary Under-Secretary, Alan Clark, during the Committee Stage of the 1984 Act, when he asserted that the central question was 'whether it is proper to give union members the right to confirm the existence of the political fund that they were originally given in 1913' [7].

The Government, then, expanded their argument from the original proposition that current members should be given the right to ballot to the notion that regular ballots should take place. There was a two-fold justification for this. Firstly, it was argued that, over a period, trade union members' political views may well change, and this was illustrated by the decline in support for the Labour Party over the previous twenty years. In addition, attention was drawn to the constantly changing membership of trade unions: a good deal of evidence indicates that trade unions are somewhat like hotels in their membership in that individuals constantly come in, and go out. Alongside a hard core of members, unions, over a period of years, will experience a significant change in the individual composition of their membership. Clark used this fact to support the proposition that there should be regular ballots: 'It is reasonable to suppose that, as a decade unrolls, a majority of trade unionists will not have had a chance to ballot' [8]. It was these arguments which the Government used to support their proposal that there should be regular review ballots, taking place at an interval of no more than ten years.

The notion of simply updating the 1913 Act was attractive to the Government, and it provided greater legitimacy than any other argument for the Government's approach. As Fatchett (1984) has commented, however, there are reasons to doubt whether the Government's arguments are based on a sound understanding of the 1913 Act:

There are no provisions in the 1913 Act for regular ballots: nor did the Attorney-General, Sir Rufus Isaacs, make any reference to regular ballots when he proposed the second reading of the Bill in 1912. There may exist, in fact, valid reasons for not providing regular ballots: the 1913 Act introduced the principle of opting-out of payment to the political fund, thereby, logically permitting, maybe encouraging, the possibility that over a period of time, a majority of members of a particular union may decide not to contribute. It could be argued that the mirror-image of the majority's right to opt-out would be a continuation of the fund to which the minority contributed: this assertion may be further strengthened by the 1913 Act's insistence that no discrimination should be practised against those who do not pay the political fund.

In addition to the Government's possible misunderstanding of the 1913 Act, there was also evidence that the provisions of the Act were working satisfactorily. For instance, in unions such as ACTT and ASTMS, it was the majority which opted out of paying the levy. In these cases, nobody argued that there was a demand for a ballot to determine collectively whether the union should have a political fund; on the contrary, all such concern seems to have been satisfied with the ability to opt out. The Government's case for review ballots was neither supported by a reading of the intentions in 1913, nor by a strong demand from unions' members.

Discrepancy

Democracy, it was argued, underpinned the requirement for a new ballot, and then for regular, periodic ballots. It was believed that a majority of trade union members might not necessarily support a decision taken some seventy years earlier. This point was stressed in the original Green Paper, 'Democracy in Trade Unions':

> It is not self-evident that a majority of the present members of a trade union in which a ballot was held many years ago would wish their union still to pursue political objects or to continue previous political affiliations [9].

The strongest evidence in the Government's mind for this conclusion was to be found in what they saw as the tell-tale discrepancy between the numbers paying the political levy, and those supporting the Labour Party. Tebbit offered evidence for this discrepancy in these terms:

THE 1984 ACT

When I see that in the North Wales area of the National
Union of Mineworkers over 99 per cent of the members
were affiliated to the Labour Party and paid the political
levy - which suggests that no more than one per cent of
them, at most, voted Conservative, SDP, Liberal, Welsh
Nationalist or anything else - I find it difficult to believe
that it was a completely free choice by the members
involved [10].

Two comments are relevant to Tebbit's statement.
Firstly, there is an inference that part of the difference
between the number of levy payers and the level of Labour
support could be accounted for by intimidation. Union
members were simply prevented from opting out. We have
seen how this claim has run through all the debates on
political funds since 1913. Always, there has been a noticeable shortage of hard evidence to support the intimidation
assertion. Tebbit, as with others, failed to provide
supporting information. Indeed, Ewing's analysis (in Lewis,
1986) of the Certification Officer's reports for the years 1976
to 1983 shows that, in total, for that eight year period, there
were only 216 complaints, of which ten went to formal
hearings, with the rest being determined satisfactorily
between the complainant and the appropriate union. The
Certification Officer's experience scarcely suggested a world
in which union members were prevented from exercising their
right to opt out.
Secondly, there seems to be a belief that there should
be a one-to-one relationship between levy payers and Labour
Party supporters. This notion was present in a good deal of
the Government's thinking, and it was based on a crucial
misunderstanding. It is rationally possible to pay the political
levy, and at the same time not support the Labour Party.
After all, the political fund is also used on expenditure other
than payments to the Labour Party; a theme which was to be
advanced very strongly during the subsequent review ballot
campaigns.

THE SHAPE OF THE 1984 ACT

The main features of the Act were predetermined by the
arguments put forward by the Government in support of the
need for legislation. For the Government it was essential that
trade union members should be given the right to say
whether they wanted their union to continue with a political
fund, and that the right should be exercised on a regular
basis. The Act determined upon ten yearly intervals with the
initial ballot, in the case of those unions which had not held
a ballot in the previous decade, which would be the overwhelming majority, to take place before April 1st 1986.

The Government, though, despite the severity of some of the rhetoric, accepted the two main principles of the 1913 Act:

a)   that, trade unions should, if they so choose, be able to pursue their members' interests through political organisations and to give support to such organisations,and
b)   that no trade union member should be obliged to support financially any political organisation if he does not want to, and that he should not suffer so far as his union membership is concerned by refraining from giving such support [11].

Having accepted those two main principles, the Government still needed to resolve its position on two questions, relating to their practical implementation. Firstly, it was necessary to decide what was meant by political in this context; and, secondly, whether it was preferable to preserve the rights of individuals by reverting to the principle of opting-in rather than continuing with opting-out.

The Definition of Political
As for the definition of political, the Government claimed, with some justification, that the 1913 Act needed updating. There was, for instance, a recognition that elections to the European Assembly should be included within the 1913 definition. About changes of this sort, there was little, or no controversy.
Where controversy did arise, however, was in relation to the addition of a new element in the definition: expenditure 'on the production, publication or distribution, of any literature, document, film, sound recording or advertisement the main purpose of which is to persuade people to vote for a political party or candidate or to persuade them not to vote for a political party or candidate' (Trade Union Act 1984 s. 17). It was the introduction of the notion of persuading people not to vote for a specific party which was novel, and which proved to be of such importance in relation to the subsequent ballot campaigns.
In the House of Commons Committee Stage of the Bill, Smith, on behalf of the Labour Party, contended that this new provision was a major extension of the application, in this context, of the term, political:

We know what that is all about. It is about anti-cuts campaigns and things like that, which are run by trade unions and which urge their members not to support a Government who are taking employment away from them. It does not say 'Go out and support the Labour Party', it says 'Do not support this Government' [12].

In what turned out to be a crucial exchange, as far as the future campaigns were concerned, the Minister was challenged about whether a campaign initiated by NALGO, against public spending cuts, and by inference, against the policies of the Conservative Government, would fall within the scope of the new definition. Whilst the subsequent importance of this exchange cannot be understated, it is initially worth reminding ourselves that the Minister responsible for answering the points implied by the NALGO campaign, Clark, felt that the campaign might fall within the definition of the 1913 Act:

> My view is that it could well fall within the present definition, although it was not actually tried in the courts [13].

If the campaign was covered by the existing definition, then, of course, it would have been necessary to pay for it through the political fund; a disqualification for NALGO as it does not possess a political fund.

If the Minister had curtailed his comments at that point, no damage would have been inflicted upon the Government's case. The Minister was, however, pressed further. He was again asked whether the changes proposed in the Bill would mean that the NALGO anti-cuts campaign would have to come out of a political fund. It was in his response to this question that the Minister provided so much ammunition for the subsequent political fund campaigns:

> The whole committee will see that this NALGO literature is as good an example as one is likely to get of something which comes into that (i.e. the new) definition (Col. 1308).

The definition of political was to be changed, mainly in a non-controversial way, but in this one vital aspect, it was to be rephrased in such a way as to raise doubts about whether those campaigns which had traditionally formed part of an accepted trade union response would now have to be regarded as political. Smith regarded the change as so fundamental that unless a union had a political fund, it 'would not have a voice about any matter of a general political or social character' [14].

There is some support for Smith's view. Ewing, (1984) for instance, makes the telling point that if the Minister's interpretation was accurate, and that the NALGO campaign would have been covered by the existing definition of political, why was it necessary to change the formula. He also cited in support of this argument the case of Coleman v The Post Office Engineering Union [15], in which the Certification

Officer held that for the distribution of literature to be regarded as political, it would have to be directly and expressly in support of a political party (Ewing 1984, p. 238).

It is also interesting to note that the commentary in the Encyclopaedia of Labour Relations Law is less than totally convinced by the Government's implied distinction between campaigning and politicking: the one could be paid for out of the general fund, whilst, necessarily, politicking required a separate political fund. Drawing the line is never easy in practice: as is pointed out in the commentary, 'like the question of a bald man, the question is one of degree' [16]. The Government, in its statements, failed to state the degree with any clarity or certainty.

It is open still to debate whether Smith's conclusion would stand up to the closest and most detailed examination, but, taken alongside the Minister's response, it succeeded in raising substantial doubt and anxiety about whether unions could behave in ways which had previously been considered as non-political. The Government found themselves incapable of removing fears that traditional trade union campaigns about jobs and employment prospects, often involving an element of criticism of government policies, regardless of which political party formed the Government, would be at risk under the provisions of the 1984 Act. unless paid for out of a political fund. These fears provided the basis of a potent theme which was to run very strongly through the subsequent review ballot campaigns.

Opting-out or Opting-in
The other main question to be resolved by the Government concerned the possibility of re-introducing opting-in. The Government's initial response was to continue with opting-out, and to rely upon the ballots as a once and for all opportunity of ending trade union political funds. This approach did not wholly meet with favour amongst Government backbenchers, and, at the Report Stage of the Bill in the House of Commons, an attempt was made to introduce the following amendment:

> Notwithstanding the provisions of the Trade Union Act 1913, all members of a registered trade union shall be regarded as exempt for the purposes of payments made to the political fund of that trade union unless they have given written notice of their intention to contribute to the political fund.

In moving this amendment, Mr. John Townend, the Conservative MP for Bridlington, relied upon three arguments. Firstly, opting-in was an essential expression of

AGE

individual freedom: 'In a free society there is no reason why anyone should give financial support to a political party unless he has expressly indicated his desire to do so. The onus should not be on the individual who does not wish to make such a payment and who, to contract out, will inevitably give other people some sign of his political beliefs. I have as yet heard no argument that deals satisfactorily with that fundamental principle' [17].

Secondly, there was reliance upon an argument which has been used in a number of different contexts: those paying the political levy far exceeded in number those supporting the Labour Party. This was construed as prima facie evidence of either, at best, bureaucratic obstruction, or, at worst, intimidation.

The third argument was, in many respects, the most intriguing. For Townend, the introduction of opting-in would severely weaken the Labour Party's finances, thereby greatly enhancing the chances of the Liberal/SDP Alliance emerging as the main opposition to the Conservatives. The singular most important advantage of this for the country, it was argued, would be that a political system would develop in which both main political groupings were committed to capitalism.

A system of removing contracting-out and removing the financial support of non-labour members from the Labour Party could result in speeding up the Labour Party's decline and its replacement by the Alliance as an alternative to the Conservative Government. The long awaited realignment of British politics would be with us. It would not just be good for the Alliance, it would be good for the country [18].

With the case couched in these terms, it is scarcely surprising that Townend succeeded in attracting the support of the Alliance parties. It was equally to be anticipated that Townend's amendment would prove unattractive to the Labour Party. The key response, then, was with the Government, and they felt that they had sufficiently defended the right of the individual. They had achieved this objective, they claimed, by providing for regular ballots.

Additionally, for the Government, the individual union members' freedom was to be further strengthened by an agreement between themselves and the TUC. Guidance was to be issued to individual members to inform them of their right to opt out. The Secretary of State, Tom King, drew the attention of the House of Commons to the Government's agreement with the TUC:

The guidance requires the unions to tell their members why a union has a political fund, to tell them what their political levy costs them, in cash terms, and as a proportion of their normal dues, to tell them that they have the right to opt-out, if they so wish, and to make clear, if they do so, that they will lose none of the other rights or benefits of members. It requires the unions to explain to their members in detail how to contract out, if that is what they want, and that information should be supplied to all new members, to all existing members after a ballot is held on the political fund, if the ballot is successful, and in addition, any member at any time if he asks for one must be given a copy [19].

The agreement, then, took the form of a practical reinforcement of the provisions of the 1913 Act. Predictably, there was opposition on the government benches. For some, it was a return to the previous bad practices in industrial relations, whereby, rather than showing determination, the Government aimed to negotiate and compromise with the trade unions. This was not seen as the Government's style.

Equally, there was criticism, and anxiety about how the deal could be enforced, and how much time must elapse before a verdict on the efficiency of the agreement could be made. The Secretary of State was particularly pressed on the question of time-scales; he was, however, not prepared to give a specific commitment.

I shall not tonight give a specific time from the Despatch Box. We are prepared to deal fairly with this matter. We shall allow the unions to make their proper arrangements. We shall be watching the position very clearly [20].

The Secretary of State's case was sufficiently strong to persuade enough of his colleagues to vote against the Townend amendment; with Labour votes combining with those of Government supporters, the amendment was defeated by 472 votes to 57. Those 57 votes, however, cast against the expressed wishes of the Government indicate the extent to which a provision for opting-in would prove popular with the Conservative party.

However, for the unions, the immediate anxiety had been lifted. With the subsequent successful review ballots, the code of practice must now be regarded as a small price to pay in order to overcome the threat of opting-in.

SUMMARY

The 1984 Trade Union Act formed the Government's third substantial piece of industrial relations legislation. All of the legislation, consistent with the overall ideological approach of the Government, aimed at reducing the power of trade unions. Unlike the earlier Employment Acts, the 1984 Act differed in two important respects: firstly, by becoming directly involved in matters of internal trade union government, and, secondly, by imposing a duty to hold a ballot about the continued existence of a union's political fund. For the reasons explained in the next chapter, the Government had cause to look forward with some optimism to those review ballot results.

NOTES

1. As a term, monetarism has been widened and popularised. In this context, we will describe it as a set of ideas which emphasise tight financial management, cuts in public spending, and limitations upon the powers of trade unions.
2. As reported in The Guardian 16th September 1978.
3. Conservative Manifesto 1979, p. 9.
4. Conservative Manifesto 1979, p. 11.
5. Trade Union Bill, Standing Committee Minutes, Col. 1153.
6. Hansard July 12th, 1983, Col. 763.
7. Trade Union Bill, Standing Committee Minutes, Col. 1220.
8. Standing Committee Minutes, Col. 1222.
9. 'Democracy in Trade Unions', HMSO, January 1983, p. 24, para 85.
10. Hansard July 12th, 1983, Col. 768.
11. 'Democracy in Trade Unions', p. 21.
12. Standing Committee Minutes, Col. 1288.
13. Standing Committee Minutes, Col. 1307.
14. Standing Committee Minutes, Col. 1310.
15. Coleman v The Post Office Engineering Union, 1981, Industrial Relations Law Reports, 427.
16. Encyclopaedia of Labour Relations Law. 2074/2. Sweet and Maxwell.
17. Hansard April 2nd, 1984, Col. 722.
18. Hansard April 2nd, 1984, Col. 725.
19. Hansard April 2nd, 1984, Col. 753.
20. Hansard April 2nd, 1984, Col. 755.

Chapter Three

BALLOTS: THE ATTRACTIVE OPTION

As the previous chapter has made clear, the Government chose ballots as the means of testing support for political funds. This chapter will discuss the attractiveness of the ballot option by reference to the Government's own rhetoric, to the decline in support for the Labour Party amongst trade unionists, and to the longer term and more significant depoliticisation of the trade union movement.

THE GOVERNMENT'S RHETORIC

We need to spend little time on this point, except to emphasise once again that the Government justified many of its trade union proposals on the basis of giving the unions back to their members. A particular view of what had happened to trade union organisation was put forward: a militant minority of activists and leaders had taken control of trade unions, thereby pushing the more moderate rank and file members into allegedly extreme and militant political and industrial stances. Whether this corresponds to reality is another question. For instance, the Association of Scientific, Technical and Managerial Staffs has often been subject to this form of criticism because, it is claimed, its overall political position is far to the left of a predominantly non-Labour voting membership. The turnout in branch elections is also extremely low, maybe offering support to the Government's implied thesis that the union has been taken over by a very small minority of activists. Undy and Martin (1984), in their study of Ballots and Trade Union Democracy, put forward a different conclusion:

> The absence of nationally organised factions and a relatively low average turnout ... suggest that ASTMS's membership is either less interested or more satisfied than its counterparts in other unions. It may well be that in this left of centre but pragmatic union the

dissatisfied members of the left, when they feel moved to protest against the leadership, find it difficult to mobilise support against the established leadership because of the 'standing' many of them have acquired having held office in the union since it was first founded (p. 90).

Maybe, then, the Government's model is not supported by hard evidence. Nevertheless, it would be churlish to deny the potency of the rhetoric. The unions, they argued, had been taken over; it was they the Government, which was to enter the fray on behalf of the disadvantaged member in order to restore and to extend democratic rights. The traditional internal procedures designed to extend and to safeguard member democracy were portrayed as irrelevant, or as open to minority manipulation. Only the Government could give the unions back to their members.

This was the justification for those provisions in the 1984 Act which dealt with internal elections and strike ballots; it was a justification which could be applied with equal force to the continued existence of political funds. For the Government, this was an especially appealing approach: against the accusation that they were attacking the finances of their main political opponent, the Government could plead in mitigation that it was simply leaving the decision to the members. It was they who would decide.

THE DECLINING LABOUR VOTE

Whilst there is little immediate evidence available to support this assertion, it is probably naive to assume that the Government did not look forward to the ballots with some degree of confidence. They felt that they had reason to expect trade unionists to reject continued support for political funds; and those reasons were to be found in the declining Labour vote amongst trade union members.

The traditional belief that trade unionists overwhelmingly voted Labour had been eroded over the previous two decades. As the figures in Table 3.1 indicate, in the seven general elections between 1964 and 1983, Labour's support amongst trade unionists has been almost halved, to reach an all-time low in the election of 1983. Furthermore, the figures do not simply show a dramatic collapse of the vote in one specific election; quite the contrary, with the partial exception of the October 1974 election, the Labour vote amongst trade unionists had declined at every single election.

Of equal interest to the decline in Labour's support was the sharp increase in support for other parties in 1983, almost wholly represented by votes for the Liberal and Social Democratic Parties. Here, again, was to be found a source of

Table 3.1:   Labour Support Amongst Trade Union Members

	1964	1966	1970	Feb. 1974	Oct. 1974	1979	1983
Labour	73	71	66	50	55	51	39
Tory	22	25	28	30	23	33	31
Other	5	4	6	15	16	13	29

Source: Taylor (in Pimlott & Cook, 1982) and Kellner [1]
          (1983)

concern for the trade unions. In addition, although Labour continued to hold the lead amongst semi- and unskilled workers, amongst skilled workers and white collar workers, the lead had been lost to the Conservatives, as can be seen in Table 3.2.

For those who wish to maintain a close relationship between trade union membership and Labour Party support, the figures in Table 3.2 must introduce a potent cause for anxiety. As the patterns of trade union membership change to reflect the contours of industrial organisation, it would appear as if the growth areas of membership include the very workers who are least likely to vote Labour. White collar members now form 36 per cent of the TUC membership; yet, it is this group which produced such a low level of support for the Labour Party that, in 1983, it was placed behind the Conservative and Alliance parties. Whilst, then, it may be desirable, indeed imperative, for the unions to compensate for their declining membership by recruiting amongst white collar workers, for the continuation of the links between the Labour Party and the trade unions, the picture was less than encouraging. At least, that was the way it seemed in the period immediately after the 1983 election, as the 1984 Trade Union Act made its way through Parliament.

Table 3.2:   Trade Unionists' Voting Behaviour by Social Class
             in the 1983 Election

	Semi/unskilled workers	Skilled workers	White collar workers
Labour	41	32	27
Conservatives	33	40	38
Liberal/SDP	24	26	33

Source: Kellner (1983)

It was not, however, only in the declining Labour support that the threat to the future political role of the unions was to be found. There was a great deal of evidence collected over more than a twenty year period to show that union members expressed anxiety about their union's political role and involvement. Some of the earlier evidence of this type was contained in the study by Goldthorpe and his colleagues (1968), undertaken in the early 1960s of the so-called 'affluent' workers of Luton. As can be seen from Table 3.3, a majority of the Goldthorpe sample approved of the viewpoint that trade unions and the Labour Party should keep themselves separate; indeed, only one group within the sample, that is, the craftsmen, approved of trade union support for the Labour Party.

Almost twenty years later, Taylor (in Pimlott and Cook, 1982, p. 194) reported a survey which showed that 46 per cent of trade unionists agreed with the view that the Labour Party should not be so closely linked to the trade unions. This is a strikingly similar result to the earlier Goldthorpe sample.

Whilst, then, there was clear evidence of a declining labour vote, and of a notable opposition to trade union links with the Labour Party, there was, interestingly no indication of either a fall in absolute terms, or in percentage terms, of the number of trade unionists paying the political levy. For instance, in the twenty years between 1950 and 1970, the total number contributing to political funds increased from

Table 3.3:

	Craftsmen (n=49)	Setters (n=23)	Process workers (n=18)	Machinists (n=41)	Assemblers (n=68)	All (n=199)
Approved of TU support for LP	61%	26%	49%	44%	37%	45%
Think TU & LP should keep themselves separate	39%	74%	51%	50%	59%	53%
Other/DK	0%	0%	0%	6%	4%	2%

Source: Goldthorpe et al. p. 111

5.83 million to 6.73 million; and, as a percentage of the total membership, those contributing to political funds rose marginally from 78.5 per cent in 1950 to 79.7 per cent in 1970. On one hand, opposition to the Labour Party may have grown, but on the other, support for the political fund had strengthened; for reasons which we have already referred to in Chapter 2, these apparently contrasting pieces of evidence may not be such a contradiction. Support for the political fund, as such, was to provide a strong theme for the review ballots.

DEPOLITICISATION OF TRADE UNIONS

For many accustomed to regular political and media comment about the power of trade unions, it may appear strange to see reference to the depoliticisation of trade unions. There are, however, grounds for putting forward such an argument, based as it is upon an apparent contradiction between the higher profile political role for trade union leaders, on the one hand, and the lack of political activity and political education at branch and local levels, on the other.

Crouch (1979), in his study of The Politics of Industrial Relations, has argued that, through the policies pursued by successive governments, industrial relations have become more politicised. This, according to Crouch, means that 'it is doubtful whether it is a matter of choice for unions whether they have a political role or not given the contemporary position of the state in industrial relations' (p. 169). It is, however, necessary to tease out the nature of that politicisation.

For almost three decades, Governments have ascribed to themselves a central role in the wage bargaining process: firstly, either directly or indirectly by being a large employer, they have been able to influence the level of pay settlements; and, secondly, through various forms of incomes policy, Governments have sought to bring their views, as an interested third party, into the wage bargaining process. In addition, Governments have been tempted by the notion that industrial relations problems, mainly as defined by reference to the incidence of unofficial strikes, are at the heart of the country's economic difficulties. If an orderly pattern of industrial relations could be achieved, it is assumed, then it is only a matter of course before economic performance improves. For this motive, Governments have sought statutory frameworks of various types for controlling trade union and collective bargaining practices. It is for this reason that the 1964-1970 Labour Government introduced its White Paper, In Place of Strife, the Conservative Government of 1970-1974 enacted the 1971 Industrial Relations Act, and the 1979 Conservative Government adopted its step-by-step approach to the reform of industrial relations.

Incomes policy and industrial relations reform bring with them a significant implication. Traditionally, the central role of trade unions has concentrated mainly, almost exclusively, upon collective bargaining. Furthermore, that collective bargaining has been defined solely in terms of wage and immediately related issues. The intervention of Government has transformed traditional practices to such an extent that what normally has been within the private domain of unions and employers has now become, to a greater or lesser extent, the subject of political interest, and, often, of political controversy. As Crouch commented, whether the state was ever totally neutral in the relations between capital and labour, the 1960s and 1970s witnessed the emergence of Government policies, which shattered any claims to neutrality.

Government intervention, it is argued, politicised a good deal of trade union activity. The depth of that politicisation, however, is of particular interest. Many commentators have suggested that trade union political involvement and influence reached its height with the 1974 Labour Government's Social Contract. The origins of the social contract can be traced to 'Labour's Programme for Britain', which was the subject of debate at the 1973 Annual Conference. 'The need is for a far-reaching "social contract" between workers and the government, a contract which can be renewed each year as circumstances change, and as new opportunities present themselves' [2].

The TUC took pride in the social contract, arguing, for instance in 1976, that it had provided 'a sense of direction, credibility and achievement' [3] to the Labour Government. Others were more sceptical, commenting especially upon the limited price which the Government appeared to pay for voluntary wage restraint. Hyman and Brough (1975, p. 107), for example, argued that 'the programme for reforms offered workers for their restraint involves only the most marginal challenge to the powers and privileges of capital: set in the context of the broad spectrum of inequality (in wealth, income and general life changes and in the whole complex of conditions, character and status of work) ... the projected measures of equalisation are modest indeed'.

In the present discussion, the content of the social contract is less relevant than the methods by which agreement between Government and workers was sought. For a Labour Government, the trade unions provided the natural vehicle for consultation, but how did that consultation work? The key question always was how far consultation extended beyond the inner circle of trade union leaders. Maybe we can find the answer to that question in the comments of some of the critics of the social contract.

Across the political spectrum, power was largely seen as concentrated in the hands of the few. Typical of the political right, the Daily Telegraph saw the Labour Government as being hijacked by powerful trade union barons; for them, Jones, then General Secretary of the Transport and General Workers Union, and Scanlon, then President of the Amalgamated Engineering Union, were 'political animals rather than economic men' [4]. For those on the left, the social contract was part of what Middlemass (1979) has defined as corporatist tendencies, controlling class conflict, and managing the aspirations of the workers. Cliff (1975), for instance, put forward the argument that the TUC leaders were conspiring with a reformist Labour Government to hold down workers' demands. He concluded that the social contract would be used to 'try to convince workers that they should not press for an improvement in living standards but aim, at best, to defend existing ones' (p. 44).

For Cliff, and many others, the social contract could not be presented as the property of rank-and-file trade union members, emerging after an intensive process of debate and discussion. Ironically, this viewpoint was endorsed by Minkin (1977), who, in countering the assertion that the powerful barons of the trade unions had taken over a Labour Government, suggested that certain guiding principles shape the relationship between union leaders and Labour governments. 'The general adherence to traditional patterns has been remarkable. Far from being hungry for power, the new generation of left-wing union leaders has proved to be restrained and mindful of wider institutional obligations.' The guiding principles, which Minkin described, did not, at any stage, include the requirement to extend political debate to rank-and-file members. Whilst trade union leaders had been brought more into political controversy, a reciprocal and supportive process had not developed with ordinary members.

We are faced then, with two sides of the coin: in the 1970s in particular, a more political leadership, co-existing with a non-political, depoliticised trade union organisation. Jones commented on the second part of this relationship, when looking forward to the then forthcoming political fund ballots. 'We have to ensure that the Labour Party and the trade unions really are bodies of participating members, rather than, in the one case, an electoral machine, and, in the other a bureaucratic organisation' [5]. The bureaucratic model, which was presumably in Jones' mind, consisted of a trade union leadership which was involved in political decision making, in contrast to the vast majority of members who were largely excluded.

If we accept that description as valid, we still have to ask why that particular state of affairs had emerged. Maybe the answer is to be found in two distinct approaches: firstly, by recognising those characteristics which form an intrinsic part of trade union organisation, and, secondly, by drawing attention to how those intrinsic characteristics have been emphasised by developments in organisation over the last thirty years.

On the more general theme, Gramsci (1955), typically of many Marxist and neo-Marxist writers, saw trade unionism as:

> Evidently nothing but a reflection of capitalist society, not a political means of transcending capitalist society. It organises workers, not as producers but as wage earners, that is, as creations of the capitalist system of private property, as sellers of their labour power. Unionism unites workers according to the tools of their trade or the nature of their products, that is according to the contours imposed on them by the capitalist system.

This reflection of the contours of capitalist society has necessary consequences for the political role of the unions. At one level, it induces a context in which the development of trade or craft consciousness is always a distinct possibility; that consciousness can, for instance, be organised around immediate economic issues, as well as towards the culture which relates to a particular form of employment. That consciousness, however, both unites and divides, with the crucial division often manifesting itself around the different economic interests of groups of workers. Against this background, a class consciousness, which aims both to unite, and to pursue political goals which are in opposition to those of capital, is difficult, if not impossible to achieve.

For this reason, it is scarcely surprising that trade unions have often been described as reactive and defensive organisations. Consistent with this viewpoint, it is always the employer who initiates, with the union reacting. In political terms, this analysis leads to the hypothesis that political activity for trade unions will be narrowly defined, with the emphasis predominantly upon the encouragement or the preservation of collective bargaining. For instance, in his study of the political activities of the Transport and General Workers Union and the Amalgamated Union of Engineering Workers, Richter (1973) concluded that unions never really depart from their concentration upon collective bargaining; political activity was secondary, mainly designed to keep governments out of industrial relations.

If the intrinsic nature of trade unionism necessarily infers a defensive and reactive role, with limited scope for politics, it must be admitted that British unionism has looked to politics and especially to Parliament, as a means of achieving gains for their members in a way which would be beyond the normal gambit of collective bargaining. These gains have rarely been predicated upon a desire to transform capitalism; the gains have been achieved as ameliorations within the framework of capitalism. This approach has been characterised by Banks (1974) as welfare unionism, which, he saw, neatly reflected in the TUC's statement of objectives to the Royal Commission on Trade Unions and Employers Associations.

In their evidence, the TUC emphasised ten aims, ranging from the immediate workplace aspirations such as improved terms of employment to broader goals such as fair shares in national income and wealth, and a voice in government. For Banks (1974, p. 63), most of these objectives were 'clearly beyond the reach of collective bargaining between employers and trade unions in the English industrial relations system. They indicate therefore the degree to which the TUC Guidelines conceive of the trade union movement in Britain as a pressure group "cause" movement.' Significantly, in operating as a pressure group, trade unions scarcely looked to their economic powers as a means of advancing their aspirations; nor was it normal practice to develop membership campaigns around political causes. Politics were largely the prerogative of union leaders and sponsored Members of Parliament.

If one accepts the more general analysis of trade union purposes, or the more specific definitions of welfare unionism, it is reasonable to conclude that political activity will be of a somewhat limited extent. It can be further argued that particular developments in both industrial relations and trade union organisation over the last three decades have strengthened the apolitical tendencies to which reference has been made.

The most fundamental change in industrial relations in the post-war years came with the conditions of full employment, as they developed in the 1950s, thereby shifting a significant element of wage bargaining away from national to workplace level. It was this shift, which led to the Donovan Report's conclusion that Britain had two systems of industrial relations, which were allegedly in conflict with one another. The formal system was structured around the national, centralised procedures of collective bargaining. The informal related to bargaining within the workplace. Whether the Donovan analysis offered much in either theoretical or policy making terms hardly need delay us in the present context [6]; what it did encapsulate, however, was the extent to which in certain industries, especially privately owned manufacturing, workplace bargaining had assumed more importance for take-home pay, and for conditions.

This state of affairs was, in so many ways, a rational response to the conditions of full employment. Employers were in competition with each other for labour. It is impossible to prosecute that competition within the straitjacket of national agreements; however, a judicious use of overtime and soft piecework times and prices made it possible to compete over the total earnings-effort bargain. In turn, of course, the employer's needs provided scope for trade union activists at the place of work, allowing, even encouraging, a symbiotic relationship between management and union activist.

Two points must be stressed about this relationship. Firstly, there emerged a growing body of union activists, usually carrying the title of shop steward, who had practical involvement in bargaining. The growth in the number of shop stewards is worth noting: Marsh and Coker (1963), for instance, concluded that the number of stewards in engineering grew three times as quickly as the growth in membership; and in a more general survey of industry, McCarthy and Parker (1968) suggested a 14 per cent increase in the period from the mid-1950s to the mid-1960s. Secondly, and maybe more importantly, whilst the extent of workplace bargaining was growing, the scope of the bargaining no more than mirrored industry-wide agreements. Wages and conditions were always going to provide the staple diet, but, in reality, little else appeared to find a place on the agenda. Managerial prerogatives were scarcely questioned, a point fully illustrated by the Clarke, Fatchett and Roberts (1972) sample of firms, in which the overwhelming majority would not contemplate consultation, never mind negotiation, in relation to those decisions which extended beyond the immediate issues of wages and conditions [7].

Many have seen in the 1950s and 1960s development of shop steward activism a reflection of an earlier shop steward movement which gained prominence and influence in the second decade of this century. In many respects, such a comparison can be misleading. For the earlier shop stewards, political ideas, especially syndicalism, provided a potent source of motivation. For the stewards of the later period, with notable exceptions, such as in the docks and the car industry, politics assumed a much lower salience. It was almost as if the trade union movement could achieve sufficient for its members without recourse to political involvement. The shift to the workplace necessarily had an impact upon trade union organisation. In certain places it brought unions together under the umbrella of joint shop stewards committees often, though, these committees did not include both manual and white collar unions, and very rarely did they succeed in overcoming the divisions which are based upon trade or occupation.

In their study of a union's response to public expenditure cuts and job losses, Fatchett and Ogden (1984) were able to draw attention to the nature of the divisions between unions even in the case of a union which had stressed to its members for a number of years the need to campaign in the local community jointly with other trade unions: 'In only 16 per cent of cases of cuts already implemented and 43 per cent of cases where branches are dealing with current proposals, have branches had meetings with other unions'. As for more general political involvement, 'there were only nine instances of a branch joining an anti-cuts campaign: few of the branches lobbying MPs, local councillors or even health authority members: and two instances where branches were planning marches or demonstrations' (pp. 223-4). This low degree of joint trade union activity, caused by inter-union rivalry, is by no means uncommon in the public sector; Fryer (1979) noted similar difficulties in the context of the campaign against cuts in public spending introduced by the Labour Government of 1974-79.

If the growth of shop steward organisation did little to lessen inter-union rivalry, it equally did little to revitalise interest in trade union affairs at branch level. Most trade unions organise their members into branches which cover a number of workplaces in a defined geographical area. This has probably always meant that branches have had limited involvement in terms of collective bargaining. Branch influence has, however, consistently been more noticeable in terms of political activities. It is through the branch that affiliation to Constituency Labour Parties and local trades councils takes place. The development of shop steward organisation constituted a parallel alternative source of loyalty. For most branches, devoid of the immediately pressing workplace issues of wages and conditions, the uneven battle was one which they could never be expected to win, or even to survive. Without ever subscribing to the notion that branch life enjoyed a golden period during which there were large numbers of regular attenders, it is, nevertheless, not too impossible to draw the conclusion that branches declined in importance and relevance from the mid-1950s onwards. In certain unions, the Amalgamated Union of Engineering Workers, for instance, that decline was officially recognised, and used as the reason to shift certain responsibilities away from branch meetings. The elections of officers, for example, which had traditionally been held at branch meetings, became subject to individual postal ballots.

Estimates of attendance at branch meetings are difficult to make. Some indication can be gained in those unions where elections are conducted at branch meetings. Undy and Martin (1984) suggested that for ASTMS the turnout for executive elections varied between 2 per cent and 7 per cent (p. 89) and for the 1979-80 executive elections in the Transport and General Workers Union, turnout was in the range of 10-40 per cent (p. 86). These figures appear to be broadly consistent with other instances of individual balloting at geographical branches.

Maybe it is not unreasonable to assert that turnout for meetings in which important elections were conducted is likely to be higher than for normal branch meetings. If this is the case, it is probably acceptable to conclude that average attendance at geographical branches often involves no more than one member in fifty.

The developments, then, of the last three decades centre upon the emergence of a body of activists, whose preoccupation has been with the workplace, where politics have taken a decidedly second place. This, coupled with the decline of the potentially more political branches, had left the unions largely devoid of the ability to mount political campaigns. This tendency has been further manifested and reinforced in other ways. As Coates and Topham (1968, p. 44) have commented, trade union information services have scarcely been modified either with changing internal patterns of organisation, or with developments in media techniques.

> Information flows are commonly inadequate in scale, so news reaches the shop floor too late, and in poor forms. They compare very badly with the fast, familiar and colloquial messages dispensed daily by the media. Trade union information conveys facts, rather than reasoning or method: what, rather than why or how, and hence induces only passivity. Members are told what to think, not what to do.

This deficiency in relation to the flow of information could have been overcome by the union's education programmes. Unlike trade unions in other countries, the TUC has so organised its educational programme that participation has been almost exclusively limited to shop stewards and branch officials. Rank-and-file members have remained largely untouched by the provision. In addition, the TUC education courses have concentrated, to a very great extent, upon technical matters, such as work study and job evaluation. The emphasis has been upon improving bargaining skills; very rarely has the bargaining process been placed in a wider political context. A possible opportunity for lay activists both to understand the broader political aims of their union, and to interpret the wishes of ordinary members to trade union leaders, has largely been lost. The picture, then, which emerges is of a trade union movement committed to a leadership dominated form of politics, which is reinforced, somewhat paradoxically, by the post-war changes in industrial relations and trade union organisation. Coates and Topham, commenting on this background, drew this very stark conclusion:

> Many British trade unions have forgotten how to organise independently (p. 43).

This view will be anathema to many whose emotional instincts lead them to expect, or to hope for more from the trade unions. They will point, with justification, to the successful campaigns in the early 1970s against the Industrial Relations Act; or to the large numbers mobilised in support of

BALLOTS: THE ATTRACTIVE OPTION

the TUC 'Right to Work March' in 1981 and the 'People's March for Jobs' in 1983. To counter this, however, one needs to do little more than look at the inability of the unions to protect themselves and their members against the impact of the recession, their inability to halt the course of a Conservative Government determined to weaken trade union power, their failure to maintain the unity of the political party which they created, with, for them, the devastating result of the 1983 general election, which nearly saw the Labour Party relegated to third place; and, above all, the demoralising experience of the 1984/5 miners' strike.

Maybe a few words about the immediate relevance of the miners' strike are necessary. Without discussing in detail whether the NUM should have held a strike ballot, or commenting upon the union's tactics, or upon the role of the police, or upon the ability of the other unions to participate in supportive industrial action, one simple but powerful conclusion emerges: the tap of solidarity, and of industrial militancy, cannot just be turned on at will, especially against a background of high unemployment.

The strike itself raised important political issues: the nature of energy policy and the relative place for nuclear energy against coal; the contrast between monetarist economics, with its sole yardstick of profitability, and, potentially a more socialist approach with an emphasis upon the relevance of a particular industry, and a positive commitment to jobs and communities. These issues rarely surfaced during the year of the dispute; the NUM's leadership on the whole appeared to demand loyalty, offering little recognition of the need to persuade others towards their own definitions of the issues; whilst the TUC and Labour Party leadership were almost wholly concerned about tactical rather than strategic considerations.

However, even if one assumes a more politically aware NUM leadership, and braver and more supportive TUC and Labour Party leaders, there is still little reason to believe that the political nature of the miners' strike would have become apparent to other trade unionists, and that they would have offered their support through sympathetic industrial action. The possible explanation for this is to be found in the widespread depoliticisation of the trade union movement to which this section has made reference. Unless one subscribes to a big bang theory of political consciousness, one can only conclude that awareness has to be worked for and developed over a period of time. Broadly, the trade unions had failed to appreciate the significance of developing political consciousness, and they had too readily accepted a division between industrial and political, in which the industrial was regarded as the main, and in some cases, only, legitimate form of trade union activity. Depoliticisation had taken a strong hold of the trade unions.

SUMMARY

In deciding upon the requirement of a review ballot, the Government had chosen an option which must have appeared especially appealing. It would not be the Government which would prevent a union from holding a political fund; that decision would be taken by the union members themselves. There were, in addition, strong grounds for anticipating a negative vote: support amongst trade unionists for the Labour Party had declined for more than two decades, whilst, at the same time, the unions had accorded a low priority to political campaigning amongst their members. The April 1986 deadline left little time to reverse the trends, with, for the Labour Party, dire consequences, if the unions failed.

NOTES

1. Peter Kellner, an article reviewing the 1983 general election in New Statesman 17th June 1983.
2. 'Labour's Programme for Britain', Annual Conference 1974, p. 14.
3. TUC-Labour Party Liaison Committee, 'The Next Three Years', 1976, p. 3.
4. Quoted in Minkin (1977).
5. J. Jones, 'The Unmentionable Menace', New Socialist, May/June 1984, p. 29.
6. For a full discussion, see D. Fatchett and M. Whittingham, 'Trends and Developments in Industrial Relations Theory', Industrial Relations Journal, No. 1, Spring 1976, pp. 55-60.
7. See, in particular, Chapter 4.

Chapter Four

THE LABOUR PARTY AND THE TRADE UNIONS

According to Pinto-Duschinsky, (1981, p. 155) 'the combination of strong union funding and weak voluntary efforts
has made it impossible for Labour to escape from its dependence upon the trade unions...'. This chapter will look at the
nature of that dependence in financial, organisational and
political terms, both at national and local levels. In order to
assess the extent of trade union involvement at local level a
postal questionnaire was sent to the Secretary of each
Constituency Labour Party, asking for certain limited and
basic data. Secretaries were asked to complete the questionnaire in the Spring of 1986, so that, with a few exceptions,
the information provided could take account of the
Constituency Party's 1986 Annual General Meeting. In total,
202 responses were received: a response rate of thirty-two
per cent (32.4 per cent). Whilst the response was somewhat
disappointing, it is not unusually low by postal questionnaire
standards; nor is there any reason to suggest that those
Constituency Labour Parties which responded were, in any
significant way, different from non-respondents.

Although the relatively low response rate necessitates
that the questionnaire data be treated with some caution, the
value of the material is to be found in the insight which it
provides in the trade union role at local level. In particular,
the information about local constituency party finances, and
the dependence upon trade union money, has previously been
difficult to elicit.

FINANCIAL DEPENDENCE

According to the Labour Party Annual Accounts, trade union
contributions represented 89 per cent of total national income
in 1978, declining to 74 per cent in 1984, before increasing
again to 78 per cent in 1985. The figures for that period are
set out in Table 4.1.

Table 4.1:   Trade Union Contributions to the Labour Party at National Level

	Total (£m)	As % of Labour Party Income
1978	1.501	89%
1979	1.842	86%
1980	2.031	80%
1981	2.509	78%
1982	2.789	78%
1983	2.969	79%
1984	2.948	74%
1985	3.496	78%

Source: Labour Party Annual Reports 1979-86

In general terms, the decline from 1978 is at variance with the previous post-war trend, which saw an increased dependence at national level upon trade union funds. There were basically three reasons for this. Firstly, the return brought about by the 1946 Act, to opting-out, resulted in a growth in political levy payers from 2.903m in 1945 to 5.773m in 1948. As far as income for the Labour Party was concerned, a similar scale of increase was evident, from £230,000 in 1945 to £466,000 in 1948. That change, of course was of a once and for all nature; the other reasons for growth are, by definition, more long term.

The first three decades of the post-war era brought with them a steady increase in trade union membership with a related and consequent growth in the numbers contributing to the political funds, as can be seen from Table 4.2.

The Labour Party benefited from the deeper penetration of trade unionism: the greater numbers paying the levy

Table 4.2:   Trade Union Political Levy Funds

	Total Trade Union membership	Total Membership of Trade Unions with Pol. Funds	Total contributing to Political Funds
1948	9.145m	7.529m	5.773m
1958	9.639m	7.735m	6.280m
1968	10.193m	7.741m	6.160m
1978	13.054m	9.888m	8.082m

Source: Pinto-Duschinsky (1981), pp. 214-5

47

enabled the trade unions to contribute more to the Labour Party, whilst, at the same time, not increasing contributions per member in line with inflation. Because of membership growth, and general inflation, the estimated total of political funds expanded from £955,000 in 1968 to just over £4 million in 1978.

In addition to these processes, it would appear as if the trade unions yielded to pressure from the Labour Party at national level to redirect resources from constituency parties to the centre. Such pressure would reflect the almost continuous financial difficulties facing the Labour Party centrally, plus an often unstated viewpoint that constituency parties might not be regarded as wholly reliable in the ways in which they would wish to spend money. Pinto-Duschinsky (1981) has described the pressure in the following way: 'Labour's National Executive Committee has for many years tried to persuade unions to hand over money to them rather than to fritter it away to various local labour causes. The argument has been that the national party is in a better position to use money where it is needed most; for example, in marginal seats rather than the Labour strongholds that have traditionally been the recipients of union sponsorship' (p. 175).

As has already been noted, the trend towards greater reliance upon trade union contributions has been reversed in recent years. Part of the explanation lies in the decline in trade union membership, and the consequent decline in those paying the political levy. This is the very opposite of the beneficial process which the Labour Party had enjoyed in the 1960s, and, especially, the 1970s. From Table 4.3, it can be seen that of the ten largest affiliates to the Labour Party, six reduced the numbers on which they affiliated during the period 1980-1983, whilst only one experienced any growth. The total net loss from these unions was just less than a quarter of a million, representing about 4 per cent of total affiliations.

Although at one level this might appear to be a small movement, when taken against previous years of confident growth, it must have caused serious difficulties for those charged with the responsibility of trying to balance the Labour Party's finances. The decline in, and the uncertainty about, trade union contributions led the national party to look to the constituencies for greater income. The 1984 <u>Annual Report</u> anticipated the greater reliance upon the constituencies: 'The trade unions, because of their large donations to the general election fund and also because of declining membership, did not feel able to increase their fees to the party this year' [1]. The constituency parties were asked to pay more in affiliation fees, and this is reflected in the fact that constituency affiliation fees, as a proportion of the

Table 4.3: Top Ten Unions: Changes in Affiliation 1980-1983

Union	1980	1983	Change
TGWU	1,250,000	1,250,000	none
AUEW (ENGIN.)	928,000	850,000	-78,000
GMBATU	650,000	650,000	none
NUPE	600,000	600,000	none
USDAW	429,000	405,000	-24,000
NUM	244,000	237,000	- 7,000
UCATT	200,000	180,000	-20,000
UCW	187,000	192,000	+ 5,000
EEPTU	260,000	180,000	-80,000
NUR	180,000	160,000	-20,000
Total Change			-224,000

Source: Labour Party Reports 1980, 1983

national party's general income, rose from 8 per cent in 1978 to 18 per cent in 1984.

Just as there is a heavy dependence of the national party upon trade union funds, so equally is it the case that an overwhelming percentage of political fund spending goes to the Labour Party. It is estimated that 88 per cent is used to fund the Labour Party at all levels, with only 3 per cent being devoted to political purposes not connected with the Labour Party. The additional 9 per cent is consumed by administrative costs, and taxation.

From his analysis of the national party's income, plus the distribution of political fund spending, Pinto-Duschinsky (1981, p. 220) felt able to draw the following conclusion: 'The variety of union giving has the practical political effect of making every level of the Labour Party organisation heavily dependent upon the unions'. Through the postal questionnaire, we aimed to achieve some indication of the extent to which individual constituency parties relied upon trade union income.

Firstly, constituency parties were asked to quantify the level of income from trade union sources. As can be seen from Table 4.4, the majority of respondents received less than £500 during the preceding financial year.

This level of trade union income tended to suggest that constituency parties were able to secure other sources of income. This conclusion was borne out when constituency parties were asked to express income from trade unions as a percentage of their total income. The results were especially interesting: only three constituency parties out of a total of

Table 4.4: Extent of Income from Trade Unions

£0-50	£51-100	£101-500	£501-1000	£1001-5000	Above £5000
No of CLPs					
11 (5.7%)	23 (11.8%)	112 (57.7%)	25 (12.0%)	11 (5.7%)	2 (1.0%)
					(n=194)

Note: (a) There were no replies from 8 CLPs
      (b) 10 replies were excluded because trade union
          affiliation fees went directly to the District
          Labour Party

177 valid replies claimed that they relied upon trade unions for more than 50 per cent of their total income.

That data hardly corresponded with Pinto-Duschinsky's assertion that, at every level, the Labour Party is heavily dependent upon the trade unions. Certainly at local level, that would not appear to apply. In order to cross check these findings, we calculated, from the information given, total income for constituency parties. This is set out in Table 4.5.

From experience, the income levels shown in Table 4.6, looked realistic. However, in order to verify further these figures, twenty constituency party secretaries were personally contacted. The conclusion which could be drawn from this additional telephone contact emphasised the reliability of the initial questionnaire returns. Constituency parties, then, seem to be capable of raising money from positive action rather than simply waiting, in a largely negative way, for trade unions to fund them. From discussion with constituency secretaries, individual membership subscriptions plus predictable, and occasionally imaginative, approaches to fund raising would seem to account for the rest of income, above and beyond that received from the trade unions. In addition, it must also be remembered that the Labour Party generates

Table 4.5: Trade Union Contribution as Percentage of Total Income

	0-25%	26-50%	51-75%	76-100%
No. of CLPs	154 (87.0)	20 (11.3)	3 (1.7)	0 (n=177)

Table 4.6:   Total Income of Constituency Labour Parties

Less than £1000	Between 1-2000	Between 2-3000	Between 3-4000	Between 4-6000	Above 6000
No. of CLPs					
18	44	39	17	24	35
(10.2)	(24.9)	(22.0)	(9.6)	(13.5)	(19.8)
				(n=177)	

income at a level below the constituency party: each
individual members' branch will raise its own money, with
probably little of that coming directly from the trade unions.
This mixture of income at constituency and local level will, in
practice, further reduce the degree of reliance upon trade
unions.

Avoiding, however, the temptation to minimise the
dependence, two further caveats need to be entered. Firstly,
it would be incorrect to conclude that trade union money is
not important, even though it may not be as important as
some have suggested. And, secondly, the questionnaire did
not permit us to calculate the percentage of total disposable
income represented by income from trade unions. A significant
element of individual membership fees is, by necessity, pre-
committed to the national party; for that reason, whilst
subscription fees must be regarded as income, they cannot be
disposed of in their entirety by the local party. Trade union
income can normally be spent without preconditions, thereby
representing a larger percentage of disposable income.

Nevertheless, on the financial influence of trade unions,
the evidence emerges as somewhat contradictory. At national
level, the Labour Party relies heavily upon trade union
funds: even taking note of the reduction in recent years,
approximately 80 per cent of income is derived from trade
union sources. The same dependence is not, however,
reproduced at local level where it would seem that the
average constituency party raises about 80 per cent of its
own income from other than the trade unions. By assuming a
national income of about £4 million per year, and calculating
from the questionnaire data, an average income of about
£3,000 per year from a constituency party, making a total
income at local level of about £2 million, it can be tentatively
estimated that some 60 per cent of the Labour Party's total
income at all levels comes from the trade unions.

Whatever additional detail needs to be added to the
calculations, it is reasonably sound to arrive at two conclusions: firstly, that without trade union funding, the

LABOUR PARTY AND THE TRADE UNIONS

Labour Party would be in severe financial difficulties, at least in the short term until alternative sources and approaches were developed; and, secondly that the extent of dependence is considerably greater at national level than at local level.

ORGANISATIONAL DEPENDENCE

In formal terms, at national level, the organisational significance of the unions can be easily stated. For example, on the Party's National Executive Committee only nine members are not totally or mainly elected on trade union votes: the seven members of the Constituency Party Section, plus the representatives from the affiliated societies and the Young Socialists. Against this group, the trade unions are able to elect twelve members of their own section of the national executive; in addition, as we shall see from the relative voting strengths, the trade unions, by their choices, will strongly influence the election of the Party Leader and Deputy Leader, plus the Treasurer and five members of the Women's Section.

A similar pattern emerges in relation to conference voting strengths. Table 4.7 sets out and compares the total number of votes for the trade unions, the constituency parties and the socialist societies at the 1984 Annual Conference.

Overall, then, the trade unions account for almost 90 per cent of the votes which can be cast at a Party Conference. The recent decline in affiliation has led to a slight reduction in the domination of the trade union vote, but, given the figures, such a decline can only assume relevance at the margins. In fact, the global figures conceal the extent to which a small number of unions can exercise a considerable influence. For instance, at the 1981 Annual Conference, the five largest unions - the TGWU, AUEW, GMBATU, NUPE and USDAW held 53.5 per cent of the total vote.

There can be, then, little doubt about the fact that the union votes dominate both Annual Conference, and the Party's National Executive Committee. Alongside this stark obser-

Table 4.7: Voting at 1984 Conference

	Trade Unions	CLPs	Socialist Organisations
No. of Votes as a percentage	6,116,000 (89.3)	663,000 (9.6)	67,000 (1.0)
Total		6,846,000	

vation, it is essential to point out that the unions very rarely act as a homogeneous group. Inevitably, political differences exist between unions, mostly upon what might be described as right-left lines, but also occasionally as a reflection of divergent occupational interests. As an example of the latter phenomena, it is necessary to look no further than votes on the question of nuclear energy: in that context, unions have supported the continuation of nuclear energy, maybe surprisingly when considered against a spectrum of other political positions, largely as a means of preserving their members' jobs.

It is, however, the left-right political divisions which assume a greater significance. On those issues, for instance, which dealt with constitutional reform within the Labour Party - reselection of Members of Parliament and the formation of an electoral college for the election of the Party's Leader and Deputy Leader - sharp divisions existed between unions. On the one hand, unions such as the TGWU and NUPE supported the proposed changes; opposing them were the AUEW, GMBATU and the EEPTU. The divisions between the unions were such as almost to cancel out the votes cast for or against change.

A further illustration of the point that it is grossly mistaken to see the union votes acting as a block is provided by the 1984 election for the post of Party Treasurer, an office determined by the vote of the whole of Conference. In 1984, there was a contest between what were largely regarded as right-wing and left-wing candidates. According to the Annual Conference records, 2.867m votes were cast by the trade unions for one candidate, with 3.207m for the other. The unions almost divided down the middle.

These examples, and very many others, illustrate how dangerous it is to extrapolate from the unions' voting strength in order to come to a conclusion that the unions can exert an overwhelming influence. Divisions will necessarily occur, although this political process does not detract from the assertion that the Labour Party is, by constitution, a party of the trade unions. It is however, within the political debates and conflicts of the trade unions that the character and the vitality of the Labour Party are moulded.

Through the postal survey, an attempt was made to assess the extent of trade union involvement at local level. Firstly, secretaries of constituency parties were asked to state how many of the delegates to the general committee came from trade union branches; equally, we sought similar information in relation to the executive committee. From Table 4.8, it can be seen that it was only in a small minority of cases that trade union delegates constituted a majority in either general or executive committees. Indeed, to some extent it could be suggested that trade unions were marginally under-represented on executive committees.

LABOUR PARTY AND THE TRADE UNIONS

Table 4.8: Trade Union Delegates as Percentage of General
Committee and Executive Committee

	0-25%	26-50%	51-75%	76-100%	
General Committee	82	102	18	0	(=202)
Executive Committee	113	80	5	1	(=199)

Although it could be argued that involvement at the
26-50 per cent level still constitutes the basis for considerable
influence, two cautions must be noted. As at national level,
there is every reason to believe that trade unionists will find
it difficult to act as a homogeneous group. Furthermore, the
size of General Committees in the sample emphasises the
intensity of the organisational skills and resources required to
bring together an effective coalition. At one extreme, there
were thirty-nine constituencies with more than a hundred
delegates, whilst, at the other, sixty-four constituencies
reported that they had fewer than fifty delegates; the most
likely size range was represented by those ninety-nine constituencies with general committees of between fifty and a
hundred.

In addition, as further persuasive evidence that trade
unions are not so organised as to exert their potential
influence, the questionnaire data showed that, in 74 of the
202 constituencies, affiliated trade unions were unable to find
sufficient delegates to fill the number of places available to
them.

As well as providing information on the numbers of trade
union delegates at constituency level, the questionnaire also
looked at the extent to which these trade union delegates
filled various offices. Again, with the exception of the role of
Vice-Chairman, trade unionists once more found themselves in
something of a minority position. For instance, in relation to
the two key roles of Chairman and Secretary, only 31 per
cent of constituency parties had a Chairman who was a trade
union delegate, and, in the case of Secretary, the figure was
even lower at 23 per cent.

There is a certain intriguing similarity for the data
concerned both with finances, and with involvement, at
constituency level. There is, in both contexts, little to
suggest that, at local level, the Labour Party is dominated by
trade unions. In few cases could the trade unionists acting as
a group outvote all other delegates; equally, there are only

54

Table 4.9: Number of Constituencies with Trade Union
Delegate as Office Holder

Chairman	Secretary	Treasurer	One Vice Chairship	Both Vice Chairships
No. of CLPs				
64 (31.7)	47 (23.3)	46 (22.7)	88 (43.5)	18 (8.9)
			(n=202)	

three cases, in which the trade unions provided more than
half the income at local level. However, having said this, it is
difficult not to recognise both in organisational and financial
terms, that the Labour Party grew out of the trade unions,
and that union influence is present, if not all powerful, at all
levels of the party.

POLITICAL DEPENDENCE

The aspects of financial and organisational influence which
have already been referred to are formal and overt. Maybe
the most significant expression of trade union influence comes
in the ability to shape the political agenda and debate within
the party.

In creating their own political party, the trade unions,
by definition, sought power through the electoral process. In
very simple terms, the electorate had to be offered a political
party which seemed capable and worthy of winning elections.
The implied notion of electability imposed certain parameters
upon the range of debate and behaviour which would be
regarded as acceptable; and, by aiming to achieve social
change from within the broad framework of a capitalist
society, the trade unions had established the limits of their
political party. This is not to assert that the boundaries were
immutable and universally accepted: deep controversies have
often arisen around topics such as the extent and the nature
of public ownership, which have from time to time strained
the boundaries, and, perhaps, redefined them. Other
aspects, however, have assumed a more permanent existence:
the rejection of violence as a means to political ends has been
a singularly important characteristic of British trade unions,
and their political party. Taken together, these mostly tacit
assumptions helped to create an identity for the party which
is acceptable, in different ways, to party members, and to
the general public alike.

As we have already seen, the unions, through the
Party's National Executive Committee, possess the potential to

exert the sort of influence which can control those aspects of debate and behaviour which might be seen to weaken the prospects of electability. That potential is further exercised in relation to the Party's Annual Conference, which provides both the best opportunity to bring to the public's attention the party's policies and values, and the risk that conflictful debate will sharpen images of division within the party.

The Conference Arrangements Committee (CAC), on which trade union representatives are not only guaranteed a majority, but, in relation to which there has been little left-right conflict between unions, is charged with the formal responsibility of structuring and controlling the conference agenda. Such responsibility carries with it an extensive power. Minkin (1980), in his study of the Labour Party Conference, provided some recent examples of the way in which that power was exercised. For instance, he drew attention to the attempts to manage the debate concerned with the possible introduction of compulsory reselection for Labour MPs; fierce 'criticism was voiced over the agenda controls exercised in connection with mandatory reselection. Supporters of reform had to fight through a range of delaying filters, including not only the three year rule, but also the rule that evolved in 1968 whereby all constitutional amendments were referred to the NEC in the first year of their submission. In spite of the weight of support for mandatory reselection it took five years of concerted pressure for this constitutional amendment to clear all the obstacles' (p. 355).

The issue of re-selection related wholly to matters internal to the Party. The powers exercised by the CAC in that example proved equally valuable in protecting the 1974-79 Labour Government from criticism from Party Conference. As Minkin commented, 'Although these technical controls operated as something of a blunderbuss they were not without political significance. In 1977, particularly, they helped save the Government from a range of defeats on the scale of 1976, and amongst resolutions ruled out of order were important critical resolutions from the Public Employees and from the Engineering Workers' (p. 356).

The influence of the CAC works to reinforce the parameters of policy and behaviour, through which trade union leaders, and the leadership of the Parliamentary Party interact to impose a significant degree of control. This process is at its most important during those stages in which policy aspirations and expressions are turned, eventually through conference debate and vote, into party policy. Minkin concluded that 'at various stages of the conference policy process there was a critical action-reaction relationship between the Parliamentary Leadership and the trade union representatives prior to the emergence of policy. Though the predominance of the Parliamentary Leadership was the most single characteristic of the process as a whole, much of what emerged as the decisions of conference, bore marks of this interaction with the unions' (p. 317).

Whilst the interaction, to which Minkin referred, serves to provide the basis of managing the party, it would be incorrect to conclude that there are not occasions when this approach breaks down. One type of situation in which that could and has happened concerns attempts by Labour Governments to interfere with what the trade unions regard as their inalienable right to bargain collectively on behalf of their members. Incomes policies, especially those in a statutory form, always carry with them the risk of serious conflict between a Labour Government and the trade unions. With the dramatic exception of the so-called 'winter of discontent' in 1978/79, attempts to minimise conflict have generally been effective, with appeals to the national interest, or the need to preserve a Labour Government in office, inducing a sympathetic reaction from trade unions.

Sympathy was largely absent, however, in 1969, when a Labour Government introduced a White Paper, 'In Place of Strife', which set out proposals for change in the system of industrial relations. For the Government what was presented as a set of beneficial reforms was seen, in contrast, by the trade unions as profoundly anti-trade union. The right to bargain was being challenged.

The main effect of the publication of 'In Place of Strife' was to unite the trade unions against the Labour Government: that unity extended beyond the usual political differences, with left and right condemning the Government's proposals. In this febrile atmosphere, the usual processes of accommodation between the trade unions and a Labour Government broke down, often into open hostility. As substantial sections of the party in general, and the Parliamentary Party, in particular, lent their weight to the trade unions' case, the Government found itself isolated. An understanding eventually had to be reached, but, on this occasion, it had to be negotiated under the full glare of publicity, rather than as a result of the characteristic processes of covert negotiation.

A further example of breakdown in the control processes can be found in the debates about constitutional change in the Labour party, which followed the defeat of the Labour Government in 1979. For many, that Government was not just defeated, but, in its policies, it had deserted many basic principles of socialism. A sense of betrayal was deeply felt, affecting trade unions and constituency parties alike. As it was the Parliamentary Party which could be cast in the role of betrayer, it is hardly surprising that those arguments seeking more accountability for MPs and the Party leadership evoked considerable support.

As the debates gained intensity, so the unions, in almost equal numbers, joined the appropriate camps, in a way in which might have been unprecedented in the Party's history, with the possible exception of the controversies surrounding nuclear weapons in the late 1950s. Traditional systems of control, and of agenda management, assumed less and less relevance. The spectator sport provided by these debates, and the organisation associated with them, became more fascinating, largely because the trade unions were unwilling or unable to reassert their control. The public might have enjoyed the spectacle, but for many, there was every reason to believe that it contributed to the decline in the Labour Party's vote at the subsequent 1983 General Election. It was the election result, with Labour narrowly avoiding being squeezed into third place, which created the necessary conditions in which a more united trade union movement has re-established, along with the Parliamentary leadership, a firmer control over the Party. The earlier primacy given to the implied notion of electability has re-asserted itself, with no better illustration of this than the well-managed and effective Annual Conference of 1986.

This brief discussion of the political influence of trade unions has concentrated upon events at national level. The processes of agenda management appear not to be replicated at local level to anywhere near the same extent. Two possible explanations can be offered: firstly, as we have seen from the earlier data, the trade unions would need to devote a good deal in resources if they aimed both to establish and to impose parameters for debate and activity at local level; and, secondly, the means of control at national level enable the unions to filter and to dilute resolutions emanating from constituency parties. There may be little incentive to seek control at local level, if with the expenditure of fewer resources, that control can, in any case, be achieved at national level.

LIFE WITHOUT THE TRADE UNIONS

We have already analysed the extent of the Labour Party's financial, organisational and political dependence upon the trade unions. The political fund ballots held out what seemed at the time, the genuine prospect of a Labour Party without the trade unions. If that development had materialised, it is briefly worth speculating as to the likely impact upon the Labour Party, and upon politics more generally.

It is relatively easy to make certain judgements. The Labour Party, at least nationally, would have found itself in a position of deep financial insecurity, with a general election at best only two years away. The cost of preparing to fight that election would have been virtually beyond the resources then likely to be available to the Labour Party.

The financial crisis may, however, have been less potent in its longer term significance than the substantial blow to confidence which would have resulted from the organised working class rejecting its formal links with the Labour Party. The claim to speak on behalf of the working class which has helped to give electoral credibility and strength, and which has also shaped working class political culture, would have sounded hollow if trade unionists had voted against continuing political funds. In a very fundamental way, the Labour Party would have changed. The loss of trade unions would have weakened, it not removed, Labour's traditional approaches to gaining electoral and political support. In addition, without affiliation, the Party, by necessity, would consist only of individuals, who, very often, by background and by political outlook, would distance themselves from working class values and priorities.

For some, this non-trade union based Labour Party would be preferable, possessing a greater potential for radical, socialist action. Coates (1975 p.v) for instance, has argued 'that Labour Party politics cannot, and will not, culminate in the creation of a genuinely socialist society; and that, on the contrary, the Labour Party and its claims are a major blockage in the struggle to create the kind of party and the kind of Labour movement that the struggle for socialism requires'. Central to Coates' hypothesis is the contention that a Labour Party, based upon the sectional, occupational awareness of the unions, is inevitably limited in its aspirations and actions, and therefore, unlikely to be an appropriate vehicle for socialist struggle. Being without the trade unions, and their innate conservatism, as defeat in the political fund ballots would have implied, could have substantially transformed the Labour Party; maybe, by applying this negative to Coates hypothesis, it would have been possible to develop a party which would be more socialist in its outlook.

Coates' critique of the Labour Party is, by no means, universally accepted. Barratt-Brown (1972), in contrast, in aiming to describe an agenda for the Labour movement in the 1970s, sought progress to socialism by advocating an approach which built upon both industrial and community campaigns. It was through those campaigns that people would become energised, and more aware of the relevance of socialist ideas. To achieve the advances for which Barratt-Brown wished, it was essential for socialists to form themselves together into a political party. He described the nature of the party in the following way: 'If this is a party only of socialists, however, it will tend to cut itself off from all other members of the groups with whom the socialists are working. In other words, a mass party is needed for building socialism in which socialists work out the details and test their theory again and again in action. Such a party would have to be based on the trade unions but also to comprehend many other single interest groups and socialist groupings that were prepared to subject their narrow interest or sectarian views to the wider judgement...' (pp. 238-9).

The differences between the positions of Coates and of Barratt-Brown are not simply limited to the practical question of whether the interests of the working class are best served by a political party developed out of the trade unions, important as that is; they also reflect a deep theoretical difference about the nature of trade unionism, and its ability to seek and to deliver socialist change. One possible outcome of the political fund ballots was to provide the conditions in which theory might be tested; an avowedly socialist party without the trade unions might have come into existence. There are sound reasons for believing that the accidental emergence of such a party would not have strengthened radical politics.

The new party would have been born not out of strength, but out of weakness. Trade unionists would have turned their back on the Labour Party, in an even more final and dramatic manner than they had in the General Election of 1983. By casting such a verdict trade unionists would have made it much more difficult for the Labour Party to maintain the loyalty of large sections of the working class. In these circumstances, especially combined with the insecurity and lack of confidence resulting from mass unemployment, and the economic recession, it is difficult to conceive of a scenario in which, in the context of defeat in the political fund ballots, the case for Labour, and for socialism would not have been seriously weakened. To strengthen further that conclusion it is necessary merely to remind oneself that, waiting in the wings, was the Social Democratic Party, buoyant after its respectable performance in its first general election, and claiming to represent all the best traditions of the Labour Party of earlier years. Defeat in the political fund ballots would have undermined the confidence of the trade unions, devasted the Labour Party, and put in reverse the arguments for radical and socialist politics; such an outcome was the nightmare that the trade union leaders dare not contemplate.

SUMMARY

This chapter has examined the extent of Labour's dependence upon the trade unions in financial, organisational and political terms. It has tried to assess that degree of dependence both at national and local levels, concluding that, whilst the significance of trade union involvement has often been accurately stated for the national level, at local level there has been a tendency to overstate the reliance upon trade unions.

NOTES

1. Labour Party Annual Report, 1984, p. 83.

Chapter Five

THE CAMPAIGN

The previous chapter has looked at the possible implications
of defeat in the review ballots. As was noted, those implications would stretch deep into the Labour Party's finances,
organisation and policy making. For the reasons to which we
have already referred, there was inevitably a certain
pessimism in trade union circles about the likely results of
the review ballot. This chapter will look at those results,
and, in addition, will describe the nature of the campaign
which prevented any of the union movement's worst fears
from materialising.

THE RESULTS OF THE REVIEW BALLOTS

The twelve months from April 1985 saw the trade unions
achieve one of their most significant successes in recent
years. By March 1986, all thirty-seven [1] political fund
holding unions had balloted, achieving a substantial 'yes'
vote, with an overall total of 83 per cent of those who voted
supporting the continuation of political funds for their union.
    Certain initial comments can be made about the overall
poll results. Firstly, in reading the results, it is impossible
not to be struck by both the depth and breadth of support
for the continuation of political funds. In only one case,
ACTT, did the level of support amongst those voting fall
below 60 per cent; even more surprising, maybe, is that only
one other union, TSSA, failed to achieve a 70 per cent level
of support. A further indication of the strength of support
can be illustrated by the fact that in six unions - ASLEF,
COHSE, NUTGW, NLBD, NUM and UCATT - the 'yes' vote
totalled more than 90 per cent of those voting. Table 5.1
fully shows the consistency of support.
    Given the consistency of affirmative support, size and
type of union made little difference to the final outcome. Of
the ten largest unions, only two, SOGAT and TGWU achieved
less than 80 per cent support amongst those voting. As we

Table 5.1:   Level of Support for Continuation of Political
             Fund

	No. of Unions
a) More than 50% and less than 60%	1
b) More than 60% and less than 70%	1
c) More than 70% and less than 80%	14
d) More than 80% and less than 90%	15
e) More than 90%	6
Total	37

shall see below, if there was a difference between smaller and
larger unions, it showed itself, not in the degree of support
amongst those voting, but in the willingness to vote.
    Furthermore, those unions whose membership could be
located either predominantly in the public, or in the private
sector, voted equally strongly for the continuation of their
political fund. Similarly, those unions whose membership was
drawn wholly or mainly from white collar workers, about whom
doubts had been expressed as to their continued enthusiasm
for a political role, also recorded substantial 'yes' votes:
APEX, 73 per cent; ASTMS, 80.99 per cent; and TASS, 76
per cent. In addition to the overall results, the other equally
striking aspect of the ballots is to be found in the unpre-
cedentedly high turnouts. Whilst the overall figure of those
voting represented 50.99 per cent of all those entitled, the
breakdown in Table 5.2 shows, for instance, that 13 of the
unions achieved participation rates comparable with parliamentary general elections.
    It is possible to draw a number of conclusions from
Table 5.2. Firstly, given the relatively high turnouts, the
unions found themselves in a position to claim even greater
legitimacy for the affirmative votes: support was achieved not
just amongst a small minority of membership, but from a

Table 5.2:   Level of Turnout in Review Ballots

	No. of Unions
30% and less	0
More than 30% - less than 50%	12
More than 50% - less than 70%	12
Over 70%	13

substantial cross section. Indeed, so widespread was the support that in the case of 20 out of the 37 political fund holding unions, a majority vote of the total membership was registered.

The turnout figures also compare favourably with other union ballots. The Transport and General Workers Union, and the Amalgamated Union of Engineering Workers held, in broadly the same period as their political fund ballots, elections in the one case for a new General Secretary, and in the other for a national President. In the TGWU, the General Secretary election produced a 43 per cent turnout compared with the 49.5 per cent of the political fund; in the AUEW the figures were 27.5 per cent for the presidency, and 37 per cent for the political fund.

Whilst turnouts compared favourably it was still noticeable that it was amongst the larger unions that participation was, generally speaking, at a lower level. Of the twelve unions which failed to attract more than a 50 per cent vote, seven had individual membership of more than 250,000. This illustrates the substantial difficulties facing larger unions: diverse membership, sometimes with different and competing interests, combined with organisational structures which often place varied emphasis upon workplace or geographical branches, tend to militate against high levels of involvement. It appears to be the heterogeneity of interest which is important; in unions like the UCW, NCU and NUM, where there is a much greater sphere of common interest amongst the members, and a broader homogeneity of organisational structure, participation rates averaged 70 per cent.

A good deal of recent interest and controversy has been aroused by the type of balloting methods preferred by individual unions. As expressed by certain sections of the media, and generally, by right wing politicians there has been a strong advocacy of postal ballots, based on two assumptions. Firstly, it is widely asserted that postal ballots will enhance participation rates; and, secondly, that the so-called silent moderate majority will be more able, and likely to impose their views by postal ballot, rather than by other methods which rely upon either workplace or branch meetings. The evidence of the political fund ballots allows us to do little more than question certain assumptions about postal voting.

The notion of a silent moderate majority is difficult to equate with the experience of the review ballots. When only two unions failed to achieve support from less than 70 per cent of those voting, and 20 out of 37 gained an overall majority amongst their membership, it is almost inconceivable to talk in terms of a silent majority. One can only assume that if such a majority existed, in relation to political funds, it must have voted yes. Indeed, Leopold's analysis (1986) suggests that 'the average yes vote for the predominantly postal ballot unions was 80 per cent compared to 83 per cent for the predominantly workplace unions'; a difference between the two balloting types of little significance or interest.

The evidence on turnout is somewhat limited, largely because of the nature of the balloting requirements. Consistent with the requirements of the 1913 Act, the Certification Officer insisted each individual member should enjoy an equal opportunity to participate in the ballot. In order to satisfy this requirement unions very often adapted their traditional practices. For instances, ASTMS, in common with many other unions, had always relied upon branch balloting. For the political fund ballot, wherever possible, workplace ballots were held, with the rest of the membership participating through postal voting. This combination became almost standard, with only four unions relying upon total postal ballot. Of these, three of the larger unions, AUEW, EEPTU and UCATT produced three of the lowest turnouts. As previously commented, size may be an important variable, but, broadly speaking, when controlling for size, and recognising the largely skilled worker base of the EEPTU and the AUEW, which could be expected to produce a higher turnout, there is evidence to suggest that workplace balloting led to a better turnout than postal balloting. Leopold's (1986) analysis confirmed this point, and he felt able to conclude 'that those unions which conducted their ballot in the workplace had turnouts on average thirty per cent higher than those using postal ballots'. This is certainly evidence which will provide the unions with useful argument in future debates about balloting methods.

So far, the analysis has concentrated upon the outcome of, and the participation in the political fund ballots, both of which can be regarded as a result of the extent to which trade unions co-ordinated a response to the challenge of the 1984 Act. It would be useful, therefore, to look at that response under three separate headings: the formal organisation, the campaign strategy, and individual union campaigns.

THE FORMAL ORGANISATION

On August 1st 1984 a conference of general secretaries, national trade union officers and senior figures in the Labour Party was called in order to consider the unions' response to the political fund ballots; in all, thirty-four trade unions were represented [2]. According to newspaper reports, the Labour Party Leader, Neil Kinnock, made clear his determination to turn the 1984 Act against the Government by using the opportunity provided to strengthen Labour Party-Trade Union bonds. Kinnock stressed:

Although we are against the legislation, which is prejudiced and carries dangers for democracy, we are taking the opportunity of campaigning with both hands [3].

In order to assist the campaign, three crucial decisions were taken or implied at that conference: firstly, to ballot; secondly, to set up a separate organisation to co-ordinate activity in relation to ballots; and, thirdly, to provide funding for that organisation.

In many respects, the decision to ballot emerged; no formal decision was taken as such. Yet, in itself, the recognition of the need to ballot was significant, and for some, it may be seen as a change of heart. The TUC was committed to a policy of non-cooperation with the Conservative Government's trade union legislation. For instance, at the Wembley Conference of Executives of affiliated unions, held on April 5th, 1982, the TUC's response to the then 1982 Employment Bill, and the 1980 Employment Act, was one of firm non-co-operation. Affiliated unions for example, were instructed not to hold or to participate in secret ballots on union membership agreements under conditions laid down in the 1980 Act, and the 1982 Bill. Further, unions were reminded that they should observe Congress policy and not seek, or accept public funds for union ballots under the Employment Act 1980 ballot fund scheme [4].

The mood, then, from 1979 onwards, as characterised by the Wembley Conference, was one of defiance. By 1984, if that mood had not changed in its general sense, there was either a change of heart, or an effective blind eye in relation to the political fund ballots. As for Part III of the 1984 Act, the TUC offered no advice as to whether to ballot. The TUC's comments concentrated upon the new definition of political; only paragraph 43 referred indirectly to the question of balloting:

The General Council note that unions affiliated to the Labour Party are jointly considering how best to campaign effectively to retain their political funds in the review ballots made necessary by the Act [5].

Maybe the TUC felt constrained from offering more specific advice or guidance to affiliated unions because only those unions with political funds were to be involved in ballots. Offering advice, then, would be aimed at only a section of TUC affiliates; furthermore, by becoming directly involved with what might be regarded as the political unions, the TUC would run the risk of losing its impartial stance in relation to party political matters.

In addition, the detail of the 1984 Act reduced the options open to unions. Whereas under the particular provisions of the 1980 and 1982 Acts it was possible, if with risk, for unions to opt out of balloting provisions, as agreed upon by the 1982 Wembley Conference, that choice was scarcely available to unions under the 1984 Act. Without the support of a confirmatory ballot, political funds would be in danger from legal action introduced by any individual union member.

For these reasons it is probably not unreasonable to conclude that the TUC felt that it would be sensible not to set out detailed recommendations; unions with political funds were to be left to their own devices to work out their own strategy.

The second decision which flowed from the earlier implicit decision to ballot was that to establish a separate body to assist in the co-ordination of the subsequent campaigns. In order to ensure maximum involvement by all fund-holding trade unions, it was necessary to establish an organisation which was broad in its membership, and not treated with suspicion because of its previous involvement in Labour Party affairs. For these reasons the existing organisation, Trade Unions for a Labour Victory (TULV), was not considered appropriate.

TULV had earlier come into existence primarily as a form of assistance to the Labour Party for the anticipated general election of Autumn 1978. In August of that year, a small group of general secretaries and presidents of the major unions met and agreed to co-ordinate union resources during the likely general election campaign, to set up a public relations unit, to pay for some advertising, and to draw up a list of speaking commitments. Not deterred by the fact that the general election was not held in the Autumn of 1978, arrangements were put in hand in November 1978 to prepare for an election in 1979. In the context of the subsequent general election defeat for the Labour Party, there is some evidence that the interventions of TULV were effective, if not totally co-ordinated. Encouraged in this way, it was felt appropriate to place TULV on a more formal constitutional basis; this was achieved during 1980.

In defining its areas of interest and involvement, TULV laid the ground for some of the criticism which was to be forwarded with some force at a later stage. For instance, TULV defined its legitimate area of interests to embrace aspects of the Labour Party's general financial income, of financial management, and of organisation. Whilst it may be possible to conclude that it was mainly the pressure of TULV which led to the establishment of a Commission of Enquiry into the Party, including four members of the TULV Committee in its membership, there was a not insubstantial number of party members who regarded the TULV involvement as less than benevolent. For these party members, TULV was seen as throwing its weight behind a particular section, at a time when internal conflict in the Labour Party was deep and passionate. As an indication of the resistance to certain proposals put forward by TULV, a suggestion to second trade union officers to examine, from a trade union perspective, party organisation at regional level was effectively vetoed. This real or perceived involvement in internal, but potentially sectional, matters disqualified TULV as the appropriate vehicle through which to organise the political fund ballots.

TULV experienced an additional weakness. Two major unions had withdrawn from membership: the National Union of Mineworkers, as early as 1980, appear to have concluded that they were opposed to the political stance of TULV, and they had withdrawn accordingly. In early 1984, the second largest affiliate to the Labour Party, the AUEW had also resigned, although, in this case, the reasons seem more obscure, and less overtly political. Nevertheless, without the NUM and the AUEW it would have proved impossible for TULV to act as the appropriate umbrella organisation.

The need for a new organisation was, therefore, acknowledged: the Trade Union Co-ordinating Committee (TUCC) combined the essential characteristics of potential breadth of membership, although in practice the EEPTU never joined, and innocence from earlier divisions and sectarianism. The structure of TUCC was simple: there was to be a Chairman in Bill Keys, the former General Secretary of SOGAT, who would be assisted by two full time members of staff. The work of the unit, which did not become operational until December 1984, was to be supported by a general management committee, consisting of General Secretaries of all the balloting unions meeting on a two-monthly basis, plus an executive committee, which would meet monthly, and which would comprise the Chairman, plus the General Secretaries of nine of the larger unions. In addition, following the national pattern of broadening TULV, the regional committees of TULV were asked to broaden their membership so as to become regional committees of TUCC. The result of this was that, as the date for the ballots drew closer, the trade unions possessed in TUCC a body with the potential to co-ordinate campaigning activity at both national and regional level.

For this campaign to look forward to the future with any confidence, there was a need for finance. The commitment to financing TUCC also came from the August meeting, already referred to. TUCC received two advances of £150,000, calculated on the basis of 3p per affiliated member. From these resources, it is apparent that TUCC was in no position to conduct a high profile and expensive media campaign. Costs were to be minimised by the central strategic decision of placing the emphasis of the campaign at workplace level. As we shall see in the next section, the strategic emphasis upon the workplace related also to other equally, if not more important considerations.

THE CAMPAIGN STRATEGY

Attention has already been drawn to the almost continuous decline since 1964 in support for the Labour Party amongst trade unionists. In addition, social survey and opinion poll evidence had also indicated majority opposition to the notion of a close link between the trade unions and the Labour Party. In this evidence were the seeds of the most crucial strategic decision which the unions had to take.

Whilst individual trade unions varied the stress upon the nature of the links with the Labour Party, the overall policy which was implemented by TUCC aimed at emphasising aspects other than the Labour Party. The campaign was not to be a referendum about the Labour Party; nor was there any requirement for the campaign to be conducted in those terms. The 1984 Act asked union members to pass judgement on whether they wished to continue a political fund. The question of affiliation to the Labour Party was a separate decision; a union can hold a political fund without deciding to affiliate to the Labour Party. Furthermore, the affiliation decision would not need by law a ballot under, say, the provisions of the 1913 Act; affiliation would normally be decided by a decision of the union conference. In addition, because unions had, in most cases, many years earlier, opted to affiliate to the Labour Party, the question of affiliation was not necessarily formally on the agenda.

It was, therefore, decided not to concentrate upon links with the Labour Party. It would, however, be incorrect to infer that the relationship between the Labour Party and the trade unions was irrelevant to the campaign. Even though the TUCC emphasised in its national guidance material that they were organising a trades union campaign, they nevertheless offered advice on how to deal, at workplace and branch level, with questions about the Labour Party. On the specific point about affiliation, after explaining the constitutional position, the advice offered the following model response:

> It is through the Labour Party that we are able to take part in making policy about the future of our industry.

> We are able to influence what Labour policies are and hence what a Labour Government will do for working people [6].

The advice concluded in the following way:

> We also affiliate to the Labour Party because we believe full employment, a strong public sector, and the welfare state to be in the best interests of our members [7].

The unions, and their active members, were therefore in a position to respond to questions about the Labour Party, and it was inevitable that such questions would arise. However, given the nature of the envisaged trade union based campaign, it was hoped to minimise the salience of such questions.

Some indication as to the most desirable strategy emerged in a private poll, conducted in the spring of 1984 for TULV. That demonstrated that, whilst only 38 per cent of trade union members approved of affiliation to the Labour Party, other aspects of political activities did not meet such opposition. For instance, 42 per cent of union members were prepared to make a 5p per week contribution towards political activities. Whilst opposition to this notion was greater, with 47 per cent opposed, there was suggestive evidence in the responses that a campaign, which emphasised the need to maintain a political fund, might strike a sympathetic chord amongst trade unionists. Even more encouraging, from a trade union viewpoint, was the majority support for the concept of sponsored Members of Parliament, acting as a voice in the House of Commons on behalf of trade union members. Of the sample 63 per cent were in favour of sponsored MPs, with only 27 per cent against.

Given the nature of the poll data, combined with the statutory requirement to ballot members on the question of political funds, the outlines of a trade union based campaign were not difficult to discern. Three main themes would be emphasised:

(i)   The right of free and independent trade unions to engage in political campaigning:
(ii)   The right to a voice in, specifically, the House of Commons; and
(iii)   The differential treatment experienced on the one hand by trade unions, and on the other by companies.

The Right to Campaign

The 1984 Act changed the definition of political. For the Government that change was regarded as little more than a necessary updating of the previous provision. For the trade unions, the new definition was seized upon as an opportunity. The exchange already referred to in which the Government Minister, Alan Clark [8], had raised doubts as to whether the NALGO campaign against spending cuts could now be seen as other than political, was reported many times, and built into an important principle.

It was pointed out that British trade unions had traditionally relied upon a two-fold approach to protecting and furthering their members interests: primarily through collective bargaining, but either when that fails, or when it is too narrow in its scope, through participation in the political process. From the very early days, that participation had always been more than merely activity in support of one political party: the objective had always been to change the political climate, and to persuade the Government to adopt policies which would be more sensitive to the interests of trade unionists.

Campaigning, then, had always formed a necessary part of trade union activity. TUCC material emphasised the historical, as well as the current dimension to the campaigning. In drawing attention to previous campaigns, two additional themes can be noted: firstly, the stress was upon the successful campaigns which the trade unions had organised; and secondly, great reliance was placed upon drawing attention to the workplace relevance of general campaigns. The necessity for political involvement in such immediate workplace issues as health and safety, pensions and aspects of conditions of employment was constantly reaffirmed.

It was, however, not the historical perspective, but the immediate NALGO example which gave such weight and credence to the discussion of campaigning. It appeared reasonable to ask about the relevance to individual unions if the NALGO campaign had to be regarded as political: did this mean, for instance, that any campaign about the privatisation of certain public sectors or activities, about proposed Government legislation like Sunday trading, which was considered detrimental to the members' interests, or about cuts in public spending with their implications for jobs and services, had automatically to be regarded as political? Certainly, if such campaigns were henceforth to be seen as political, then the almost universal practice of financing out of the general funds would no longer be available.

The conclusion was set out in the campaign literature: if you want your union to continue to enjoy the ability to represent your interests in ways other than collective bargaining, then you must support the continuation of the political fund. In practice, this proved to be a strong argument. It was further reinforced by the almost endless ability to come up with examples from each individual union; and by the unmeasured but apparent conclusion that the majority of trade union members supported in principle the general need for political campaigning. In this respect, the unions were emphasising an argument which evoked significant resonance with their members.

A Voice in Parliament
Against a background of substantial support for sponsored MPs, it is scarcely surprising that their role was given a certain prominence. Individual unions often produced leaflets containing photographs of, and biographical material about their sponsored MPs. These MPs were the voice of the union in Parliament, representing all the union's members.

In their background brief, the TUCC spoke of sponsored MPs in the following terms:

> Their first duty of course is to their constituents and the union recognises this. But they also put the point of view of our members directly in Parliament. As MPs, they have been able to reflect the unions' industrial and occupational interests at all the important decision making levels in Parliament: union MPs can also help individual union members, not least where the local M.P. is unsympathetic to trade unionists [9].

Sponsored MPs, then, were a resource available to the union, and to all its members. In relation to the political fund campaign, individual unions adapted their experience of sponsorship in order to draw attention to relevant experience and issues. A common thread emerged, however. It was again considered both desirable and necessary to state the immediate individual and workplace relevance of sponsored MPs. The resource was of even greater value, if it could be demonstrated that it was of direct benefit. It was, therefore, essential to offer examples of sponsored MPs, through Parliamentary question, speech, or proposed legislation, aiming to further the interests of union members. Beneficially for the campaigns, such examples were not too difficult to find.

Fairness
Since the 1913 Act, trade unions have been obliged to differentiate between their political and industrial functions. In order to engage in what Parliament deemed political, it was necessary to establish a political fund, following an affirmative vote by the membership. The 1984 Act added to the conditions laid down in 1913, by imposing the requirement of regular ballots. Given these constraints, it was an irresistible temptation for the unions to compare the manner in which they were treated with the treatment enjoyed by companies. Overtly, companies intervene in the political process. In 1984, they donated £2.8m to the Conservative Party, and to associated right-wing organisations; in addition, a small amount was contributed to the Social Democratic and Liberal Parties.

These company contributions differed from their trade union equivalent in a number of ways. Firstly, there was no requirement for a company to distinguish between its normal trading activities and its political functions. Using the trade union analogy, political activities were being paid for out of general funds.

Secondly, there was no need for any effective process of accountability either upon the policy decision which brought an individual company into the political arena, or upon the individual decision to donate to a political party or political organisation. Again, that could be contrasted with the statutory need for unions to ballot their members before establishing a political fund.

Thirdly, whilst the 1913 Act provided the facility for individual trade unionists to opt out of paying the political levy, no similar facility was offered to either shareholders or employees of companies. Notwithstanding the practical and technical difficulties involved in providing rights for share-holders and, even more so for employees, there still appeared to be more favourable treatment of companies than trade unions.

It can be argued that the disparity of treatment between company and union had existed since 1913, without necess-arily arousing strong emotions. Indeed, in their own ways, the practices of trade union affiliation, on the one hand, and company donation on the other, had become an accepted part of the post-war political consensus. That consensus, however, had been transformed by the policies of the Conservative Government and by the specific details of the 1984 Act. Traditional unfairness was now being added to, and, at a time when the trade unions felt that their political voice was being silenced.

An additional twist to the unfairness argument was provided by the possibility that trade unions might lose their sponsored MPs, whilst, at the same time, the number of company directorships and consultancies held by Conservative MPs seemed to grow. According to the 1986 Register of Members' Interests, Conservative MPs held a total of 618 directorships and consultancies. This evidence clearly suggested that the company voice would continue to be heard in Parliament. This provided another powerful argument upon which to ask trade unionists to continue to support their unions' political fund.

INDIVIDUAL UNION CAMPAIGNS

The existence of the TUCC guaranteed both that there would be a general shape to the campaigns, and that individual unions would lose much of their usually jealously guarded autonomy. The overall campaign developed its character through certain strategic decisions: that it would be trade union and workplace based; that standard material would be developed, aimed at individual trade unionists in the place of work, with the emphasis upon the case for maintaining a political voice; and that, at regional level, through the TUCC, individual unions would inform and support each other, with a view to achieving some degree of co-ordination. Flowing from these particular decisions was another concern-ing the timing of balloting.

Two alternatives were possible: either a 'big bang' general election in which all the unions held ballots at the same time, or a phased approach. The general election concept was soon dismissed, as it was felt that such a campaign ran the pronounced risk of the issues becoming much more party political, with the question of affiliation to the Labour Party assuming a high profile. Furthermore, it was considered that the influence of the media would be at its greatest, and, from a trade union viewpoint, at its most malign in the context of a simultaneous campaign. Media interest and resources were likely to wane, and to be dissipated, if unions took advantage of the time available until March 1986.

On the other hand, a phased approach required some discipline and co-ordination. Given the nature of trade union organisation, it was impossible to envisage the TUCC as a central body, with the powers necessary to dictate a timetable to individual unions. There was, however, a common fear of losing the political funds, and this fear injected an understanding of the need for self-discipline. There was additionally a recognition that, for a phased approach to be effective, rather than in the worst possibility, a long running bad dream, it was necessary to ensure that unions with the strongest chance of success should ballot early, thereby establishing an overall beneficial climate. Whilst those directly involved may not have seen a close correspondence between what might have been an ideal sequence of balloting and that which emerged in practice, there was sufficient likeness to make it possible to imply a strategy. It was, as we know, an effective approach, because, as time passed and the early results provided conclusive affirmative votes, there was less interest shown by the media in the possibility of individual unions losing their political funds.

The approach was equally effective in another respect: common themes and material were widely used, helping, as a result, to develop a marked similarity about the campaigns. Because of this similarity, there seems little purpose served in dwelling too long upon individual examples. However, it might be useful to look at three unions, the TGWU, NUPE and ASTMS in a little detail. The reason for selecting these three unions is that, in one case, the TGWU, the campaign conformed closely to the national pattern, whilst in the other two cases, for different reasons, there was a marked difference from the general approach.

The Transport and General Workers Union (TGWU)
The importance of the TGWU can scarcely be overstated. Its total membership represents about 15 per cent of union membership affiliated to the TUC, and its political levy paying membership just less than a quarter of the total affiliation to

the Labour Party. Defeat in the TGWU ballot would have sent shock waves through the whole labour movement.

It had been the TGWU which had led, with some passion and vigour, opposition to the Conservative Government's trade union legislation. The TGWU had also been instrumental in developing the tactic of non-cooperation with the balloting requirements of the Government's legislation. Despite this, and in common with other unions, there appears to have been little concerted opposition to the acceptance of the need to ballot in relation to the political fund.

Initially, perhaps, approval of balloting was implied: through the involvement of the union's political officer in the background work which led to the formation of TUCC; through participation at senior level in the August 1984 conference which gave formal approval to TUCC; and through the decision to provide for TUCC accommodation and other resources at the union's headquarters. Against this background, perhaps the only surprise is that it was not until December 1984 that the union's national executive took the decision to ballot.

What followed subsequently is typical of the thorough approach adopted by the unions. In January 1985, a conference of the union's regional and national secretaries was held in order to prepare and to approve the guidelines for the subsequent campaign. Again, as with other unions, the emphasis was to be upon the workplace. For those closely involved, this differentiated the political fund campaign from earlier campaigns: instead of simply organising meetings which would attract only the activists, the objective on this occasion was to ensure that the propaganda message was presented in an effective form to as wide a spectrum of members as possible.

With this aim in mind, a broad programme was developed, which sought to ensure that the focus was at regional level, therefore building upon the union's organisational strength and local knowledge, with the union nationally providing the necessary support and co-ordination. This national role showed itself in a number of ways: by providing an activists' guide, which sought to assist those who were likely to play key lay roles; by developing in liaison with the regions, and with the trade groups, general and specific material; and by encouraging participation in the specific education provision provided by either the union itself or through the education services of the TUC.

As might be expected given the strong links between the TGWU and the TUCC, there was a marked TUCC influence upon the campaign material. Around the themes of keeping a voice, distinct leaflets were produced for individual trade groups, and an additional separate leaflet for the union's women members. In this way, it was hoped that the message would be sufficiently targeted to reach the many different interests which are represented by the TGWU.

The early certainty of the campaign was shaken by the emerging controversy about the conduct of the union's General Secretary election. When it was decided that it was necessary to re-run the General Secretary ballot, the initial timetable for the political fund campaign had to be amended, firstly, it seemed, to the possibility of holding the ballot in early 1986, and then, finally, after the decision of the National Executive in July 1985, to allow for a ballot in September 1985. Despite the additional work which the alteration in timetable involved in relation to the campaign, there appears to have been no noticeable adverse impact.

A substantial problem did, however, emerge. When the decision was taken to ballot, there were no agreed rules as to its conduct. As with other unions, the rules had to be agreed with the Certification Officer. Negotiations took place during August 1985, with agreement being reached only a matter of days before the proposed September starting date. The main stumbling block was a direct result of the General Secretary elections: there had been a court decision which, in relation to the re-run of the General Secretary election, had affirmed the requirement for both a count, and an announcement, at each individual branch. For the political fund ballot, in which the union used a preponderance of workplace balloting, supported by postal voting, the Certification Officer was prepared to accept a regional count.

As Appendix 1 shows, the TGWU achieved a substantial affirmative vote. Apart from the general favourable climate in which the ballot was held, some explanation of the success must be attributed to the close adherence of the TGWU to the overall TUCC strategy: the emphasis was upon keeping the voice, amending that message to the union's diverse membership, and upon presenting the arguments effectively in the workplace. In these respects, the TGWU was almost a model union for the TUCC.

NUPE and ASTMS

Both NUPE and ASTMS diverged to a substantial extent from the TGWU. In NUPE's case, the interest lies in the length of campaign, and the degree of emphasis upon links with the Labour Party.

It was as early as November 1984 that NUPE's Executive Council decided to conduct a ballot, and, about a month later, the union's General Secretary wrote to all branches informing them of the decision to ballot. The campaign, which lasted for more than ten months, was deliberately prolonged, as this was regarded as the most effective means, not just of winning the ballot, but of building up workplace organisation, and promoting education and political discussion. Three phases of the campaign were planned. Firstly, it was necessary to prepare the ground both organisationally, in the sense of undertaking the bureaucratic tasks essential for the conduct of the ballot, and politically: the political emphasis was upon awakening members to the purpose of the ballot and to the arguments in favour of a 'yes' vote. In addition, more intensive educational work was organised with the union's branch officials and stewards so that they would be better able to carry the union's case to the members. The second phase was seen in terms of winning the members. This was a period of intense campaigning, centred around workplace meetings and discussion, and the wide distribution to individual members of the campaign material. Finally, the third phase aimed at ensuring the maximum participation in an efficiently conducted, largely workplace ballot.

The main interest in relation to NUPE lies not just in the length of the campaign, but in the nature of the arguments used to support the continuation of the political fund. Inevitably, there was reference to fairness, and to the need for a voice; but, in NUPE's case, unlike other unions, there was a much closer identification with the Labour Party. For instance, in the leaflet which went to particular sections of the union's membership - in health, local government, water and the universities - there were references to the damaging impact of the policies of the Conservative Government, and to the benefits of affiliation to the Labour Party. This was further reinforced in the General Secretary's letter to all individual members, asking for their support, in which he argued that the union's political fund allowed the union to work with the Labour Party in order to obtain a better deal for NUPE members. In this example, the Labour Party was, if not up front, certainly prominent, and this was seen by the union's senior officials as necessary for, and consistent with, the objective of securing greater involvement in the Labour Party through more branches affiliating, and sending delegates, to their local Labour Party.

ASTMS's approach to the review ballot offered, in a number of ways, a sharp contrast with that of NUPE, and, indeed with virtually every other union. Firstly, after an initial involvement with TUCC, ASTMS decided to distance themselves and to run their own campaign. It was felt that, given the union membership's minority support for the political fund, and for the Labour Party, it would be preferable to determine upon a campaign which related wholly and directly to the particular needs and priorities of the union's members. Secondly, again unlike NUPE, and certain other unions, it was decided that the emphasis of the campaign should be upon aspects other than affiliation to the Labour Party. In this context, substantial weight was accorded to the role of the union's parliamentary committee, which is made up of MPs who are also union members. The parliamentary committee, it was argued, could only perform its role as a valuable addition to the union's collective bargaining functions if the political fund continued to exist. Consistent with the earlier TULV poll evidence which showed a noticeable degree of support for the notion of sponsored MPs, ASTMS was able to command similar sympathy for the work of its parliamentary committee. And, thirdly, ASTMS resolved to conduct their ballot over a period of more than six months, thereby, hopefully, minimising the opportunities for concerned opposition. Taking into account the earlier media interest in the possibility that the ASTMS review ballot may not produce majority support, a campaign spread over a number of months appeared to be a sensible strategy. In addition to the timescales, the normal procedures for balloting in the union were altered, so that instead of conducting branch ballots, a mixture of workplace and postal ballots was adopted. It was considered that the workplace would offer a useful opportunity to state the case for retaining the political fund.

As the results in Appendix 1 indicate, the ASTMS strategy was particularly effective, with a vote in favour of retaining the fund not dissimilar to that of NUPE. The conclusion which can be drawn, is that, whilst the TUCC guidelines constituted an overall viable approach, individual unions adapted that model, to a greater or lesser extent to satisfy their own needs, without necessarily altering the general pattern of results.

THE CAMPAIGN AND THE POLITICAL PARTIES

For their different reasons, all the main political parties had a direct interest in the result of the review ballots: for the Labour Party, that interest was financial and organisational; and for the Conservative, Liberal and Social Democratic parties, there was the possibility and the hope that one of their main opponents would be severely, if not mortally, damaged. At national level, the Labour Party's involvement was in accord with the strategy and wishes of the TUCC. There was no attempt to use the campaign as a party political platform. There were, for instance, no national rallies, nor dramatic personal interventions by the Party Leader, or other key Party figures. The emphasis upon the trade union dimension, and, wherever possible, upon the workplace, was accepted. Typical of that acceptance was the role played by individual sponsored MPs. The perceived positive benefits for individual trade unionists, as indicated by the opinion polls, suggested that the campaign would gain by using sponsored MPs in such a way as to emphasise their trade union contribution rather than their involvement in party politics.

The concept of, and the need for, a trade union based campaign seems to have been equally accepted at constituency party level. As part of the postal questionnaire, constituency party secretaries were asked to state the level of involvement in the review ballot campaigns. The question was open-ended, and the answers have been grouped to show a range of activity, from no involvement at one extreme to some participation in campaigning. The most striking conclusion is that the review ballots virtually passed by Constituency Labour Parties, without a great deal of contact between unions and Party. Two explanations can be advanced for this: firstly, it was felt that it was appropriate for the Party not to be involved, as the emphasis had been placed upon a trade union campaign; and, secondly, the impression was conveyed, in responses, that other matters, maybe local elections or issues internal to the Labour Party, were considered to be of greater importance. Also, because of the nature of the campaigns, spread over a period of months, it was always likely that the involvement of local Labour Parties was going to be marginal. Table 5.3 endorses this conclusion.

The Government, and, by definition, the Conservative Party had set the rules for the political fund ballots. Whilst formally the Government had always repeated its view that it only wished to update the balloting requirements, there remains little scope for doubt that many Conservatives looked forward with some relish to the prospect of the members voting away their political role.

Consistent with that wish was the initial intervention by the then Secretary of State for Employment, Tom King. In a press statement on the day before the political fund provisions came into force, King offered the following advice to trade unionists:

Table 5.3: Constituency Labour Party Involvement in Review Ballot Campaigns

No involvement	44.6%
Internal party discussion but no external activity	31.2%
Offered assistance but not taken up	6.9%
Offered assistance including facilities and taken up	6.9%
Involved in Trade Union campaign work	8.4%
No response	2.0%
(n=202)	

Vote whichever way you wish but make sure you know what you are voting for. And that quite clearly is the question: 'Do you want your union to engage in party politics?' [10].

Dismissing the argument that the new definition of political contained in the 1984 Act meant that a political fund was now required to pursue traditional trade union activities, King stressed again what he regarded as the basic question:

Do union members want their leaders not only to spend money but also to dissipate time and energy in playing party politics; or do they want them to get on with the important job which trade unions were set up to do - representing their members' interests? [11].

Those organising the TUCC campaign would not accept the distinction which King implied: for them, the issue was about protecting traditional rights, and not about party politics. The effectiveness of the TUCC campaign can be found in their ability to secure that issue as the one of prime importance; the Secretary of State's failure to inject a party political dimension shaped the future reaction of the Government.

As a succession of 'yes' votes was recorded, the Government relied upon the argument that it was content with the important exercise of democracy: the outcome of that exercise was of limited interest to them. However, that position appears difficult to sustain when read against the comments of the Employment Minister, Mr. Peter Bottomley, who, at that stage, was commenting upon the first twenty-seven ballots. Bottomley complained:

The campaign that the TUC has been co-ordinating has been less honest. Some unions have failed to make it clear that they only need a political fund if they wish to spend money on party political or electoral matters. They have misrepresented the changes made by the 1984 Trade Union Act to the definition of 'political objects'. That legislation did no more than clarify and bring up to date the definition provided by the Trade Union Act of 1913. They have argued misleadingly that unions' ability to campaign on their members' behalf will be constrained without a fund. They have omitted to tell their members how much of their political funds go directly to the Labour Party [12].

This criticism of the trade union campaigns was probably little more than an indication that the Government had become a victim of its own strategy. By changing the definition of political, the Government had offered a campaigning opportunity which was legitimately and effectively taken up by the unions. It is inconsistent to complain about that, when one claims, as the Government did, that the sole purpose of the exercise was not to attack your main political opponent but simply to offer trade unionists the opportunity of deciding whether they wanted to continue with a political role for their union.

Partly as a result of its own inconsistency, and partly because of the strong support shown in the ballots for a continued political role, the Government became more and more cast in the role of spectator. Equally, this was true of the Conservative Party's own trade union organisation, the Conservative Trade Unionists (CTU). For the CTU to adopt an energetic stance against political funds may have embarrassed its own Government, which professed indifference. There is, also, evidence that, according to the leaders of the CTU, they lacked sufficient resources to mount an effective campaign against retaining their political funds. That concern about limited resources also implied a willingness on the part of the CTU to campaign. One senses, however, that a similar enthusiasm never existed in the higher echelons of the Conservative Party, largely because to display such keenness would expose the Government to the accusation that it was involved in party politics; and that its real objective was to inflict damage upon the Labour Party.

Such questions and hesitations did not exist for the Alliance Parties. For them, the vision of a Labour Party without the trade unions provided a genuine opportunity. Recognising that opportunity was easy; deciding how to respond effectively was much more difficult. A number of themes emerged in the Alliance response. Firstly, there was an intervention through the President of the SDP, Mrs. Shirley Williams, in which she pledged that her party would campaign for a 'no' vote, unless the unions agreed in each case to a further ballot about whether they should affiliate to the Labour Party. The Liberal Party Leader, Mr. David Steel, put forward a similar argument in a letter to the TUC General Secretary: a somewhat unfortunate intervention as the TUC itself had no political fund, and as it numbered within its affiliates non-fund holding unions.

Hardly to anyone's surprise, the offer made by the Alliance Parties was rejected, without any suspicion of interest. At that stage the Liberals and the SDP committed themselves to campaigning for a 'no' vote. Apart from some initial newspaper advertisements, and fringe meetings organised at certain trade union conferences, the Alliance involvement scarcely caused a ripple upon the calm waters enjoyed by the TUCC. Maybe because of limited resources, but much more likely because of the failure to understand the prevailing mood, the Alliance quest for a 'no' vote was scarcely heard of after the first few months of balloting.

In addition to their support for a 'no' vote, the Alliance parties took the opportunity offered by the ballots to reaffirm their support for opting-in, rather than opting-out of the political levy payment. Mr. Alan Beith, a Liberal Member of Parliament, introduced a Bill, designed to enact the principle of opting-in [13]. The arguments employed were similar to those used at an earlier stage in relation to the 1984 Trade Union Act; as on that occasion, they failed to find a majority in the House of Commons. This exercise was, no doubt, regarded by the Alliance parties as a useful early intervention in the political fund ballots.

SUMMARY

This chapter has concentrated upon the nature of the fund campaigns. A clear conclusion has emerged: the trade unions felt that it was strategically necessary to run a campaign which was based upon the workplace, and which stressed the advantages to individual members of their union having a political role. The unions succeeded in this objective with two logical consequences: firstly, there was an inevitable broad similarity in the campaigns of individual unions, with stress being laid upon the same themes; and, secondly, by emphasising the trade union nature of the campaign, party politics and political parties were largely excluded.

NOTES

1. All references are to the thirty-seven unions, with membership throughout the United Kingdom. In addition, a review ballot was conducted by the Scottish Carpet Workers Union, which, as the name implies, recruits only in Scotland. The results of the SCWU ballot are included in Appendix 1.
2. See The Daily Telegraph, 2nd August, 1984.
3. As reported in The Times, 2nd August, 1984.
4. 'Industrial Relations Legislation: The Employment Act 1980 and Employment Bill 1982', Report by the TUC General Council, adopted by the Conference of Executives of Affiliated Unions at the Wembley Conference Centre on April 5th, 1982.
5. TUC, '1984 Trade Union Act: The Trade Union Response to the New Legislation', adopted by The General Council, August 1984.
6. Quote from TUCC guidance material which was made available to every union.
7. Quoted from TUCC guidance material.
8. See for a fuller discussion, Chapter 2.
9. TUCC guidance material.
10. Press Notice, The Department of Employment, March 30th, 1985.

11. Department of Employment, March 30th, 1985.
12. Press Notice, The Department of Employment, December 19th, 1985. It is interesting to note that the Minister referred incorrectly to the TUC and not to the TUCC.
13. Hansard, April 3th, 1985. Leave to introduce the Bill under the Ten Minute Rule provision was refused by 139 votes to 68.

Chapter Six

EXPLANATIONS AND IMPLICATIONS

As the political fund campaign progressed, a certain smoothness and inevitability developed; the campaigns flowed assuredly towards a strong affirmative vote. Blessed with the wisdom of hindsight, trade union leaders may express little, if any, surprise with the eventual results. Yet, when compared with the initial polls taken for TULV the eventual outcome can be regarded as little other than a success in defining the issues, and in basing an effective case upon those issues. Some explanation of that success is necessary; as is a discussion of the implications which flow from the success.

SOME EXPLANATIONS

In Chapter 3, we developed the argument about depoliticisation in relation to the trade unions. It was stated, for instance, that the process of depoliticisation had taken place over, at least, two decades. Yet, during a period of less than twelve months, the unions were able to achieve substantial support for the proposition that they should retain their political funds. Superficially, there appears to be some contradiction between, on the one hand, the argument about depoliticisation and, on the other, the experience of the review ballots. One possible explanation might have been found in a sudden surge of support for the Labour Party, and, by implication for the link between the party and the unions. However, according to MORI, even though the Labour Party held a lead over both the other two parties in seven out of the twelve months of the review ballot period, and led the Conservatives, but not the Alliance, in one other month, its popular support never exceeded more than 38 per cent of those expressing voting intentions. This is scarcely the sort of evidence which leads to the conclusion that there was such a strong pro-Labour tide in the country that it swept the political fund ballots along with it.

There may, however, be an alternative interpretation of the voting intentions data, set out in Table 6.1. For instance, it could be argued that, in each of the twelve months covering the period of union ballots, there was a substantial anti-Conservative majority, varying from 70 per cent to 62 per cent. As it was a Conservative Government which introduced the requirement for periodic political fund ballots, it might be suggested that the anti-Conservative majority, which would be proportionately greater amongst trade union members, might take the opportunity of voting against the Government. Whilst there is a superficial attraction to this argument, it is weak in a number of respects. Firstly, as we have seen in the previous chapter, the Conservative Party and the Government mostly adopted the public posture of being indifferent to the results of the ballots, as their concern for the desirability of periodic ballots had already been satisfied. This led to a low profile, and presumably, a reduced opportunity to stimulate an anti-Conservative vote. Secondly, it is necessary to recognise that the anti-Conservative majority was divided, with the Labour Party earnestly wishing for the continuation of trade union political funds, and with the Alliance Parties putting forward a more ambiguous message, with their support being conditional upon a future ballot about political affiliation.

If the explanation of the results cannot be found in a pro-Labour tide, or anti-Conservative majority, other approaches might prove more profitable. Spencer [2], in a small, but interesting survey of Tees-side steelworkers, has come forward with some persuasive material.

Table 6.1: Political Trends: April 1985 - March 1986, Voting Intentions

	Labour	Conservative	Alliance
April 1985	37	38	24
May	35	33	30
June	36	35	27
July	34	33	31
August	35	31	31
September	33	30	35
October	36	37	25
November	36	36	25
December	35	35	28
January 1986	38	33	28
February	35	34	30
March	36	34	28

Source: 'British Public Opinion': March 1986 [1]

Attention has already been drawn to the extent to which the TUCC decided upon stressing the need for, and the value of, trade union members having a voice in Parliament. In Spencer's example, 83 per cent approved of a distinct voice in Parliament; a figure which intriguingly corresponded with the number in the sample which said that they intended to vote 'yes' in the subsequent ballot, and which was extremely close to the eventual outcome in which 85 per cent of those who voted in the union overall supported the political fund. The attractiveness of the concept of a voice may clearly have extended beyond this sample of Tees-side steelworkers: in the Iron and Steel Trades Confederation, of which this group was in membership, fewer voted against continuing political funds than, at that time, opted out of paying the political levy. This pattern was reproduced in eight out of the thirty-seven fund holding unions. Table 6.2 provides examples of that pattern.

The examples in Table 6.2 can lend themselves to a number of possible interpretations. Firstly, as Spencer has indicated, the argument about a voice appears to have been well chosen, and to have evoked a sympathetic response. Secondly, there is the two bites of the cherry argument. If you wish to opt out of paying the political levy, you are granted the facility to do so by Parliament. If, however, you both exercise your right to opt out, and, in addition, you vote, along with a majority, to discontinue the union's political role, you succeed in preventing those who wish to contribute financially towards a political role from doing so. Maybe this argument did not persuade many to vote in favour, even though they presently opt out, but it was often used during the campaigns.

In addition, and as we saw in the debates during the passage of the 1984 Trade Union Act, there were often

Table 6.2: A Comparison of Those Voting 'No' and Those Opting Out

	Number Voting No.	Number Opting Out	Col. 1 as % of Col. 2
UCATT	5,295	88,873	5.9%
EEPTU	26,830	109,787	24.4%
AUEW ENG.	44,399	400,954	11.1%
GMBATU	54,637	115,331	47.4%
SOGAT	25,947	95,463	27.2%
COHSE	7,731	19,139	40.4%
NUM	9,958	117,631	8.5%
USDAW	17,824	33,899	52.6%

implied suggestions that opposition to union political funds embraced a significantly larger percentage of union membership than simply those who were prepared to state openly their opposition by deciding to opt out. The evidence of the ballots casts a certain doubt about this proposition, even though there are examples of unions in which more members voted 'no', than opted out. The Transport and General Workers Union, in which 119,823 voted 'no', as against 29,661 opting out, and the National Union of Public Employees in which 18,310 opted out, in contrast to the 60,332 no voters, fall into this category. This group of unions is, however, in a minority, with only thirteen instances out of thirty-seven.

Spencer's data also offers a fascinating insight into the motives of those who opt out, and those who pay the levy. There is, as might be anticipated, no neat relationship along the lines of political support or opposition. For instance, Spencer found that, amongst the casting crew, 7 per cent more were prepared to pay the levy than actually favoured having a voice in Parliament. In contrast, amongst those working at the finishing end of the plant, 90 per cent wanted a voice in Parliament, but only 65 per cent were prepared to pay. Whatever the motives for deciding whether to pay the levy, there is little evidence either from Spencer's sample, or the ballot results in general, to conclude that there is a substantial pool of members wishing to opt out of paying the levy, but, for some reason, prevented from doing so. This observation is, furthermore, consistent with the failure of previous attempts to bring forward evidence of ·intimidation in relation to paying the levy.

In many respects, the obvious explanation of the ballot success is the most powerful. The unions defined, through the initial polling material and through the emphasis in the subsequent campaigns, the issues to which their members would respond positively. There was support for having a voice in Parliament, for sponsored MPs, and for the ability to advance the members interest by means other than collective bargaining. The success of the TUCC, and its individual unions, is to be found in their ability to identify those arguments to which their members would respond positively, and, then, to build their campaigns around those themes.

It is in the nature of that success that the apparent contradiction between the depoliticisation thesis, and the review ballot results can be explained. The success was built upon a sensitive recognition of the members' interests and priorities: no action on the part of the individual member or cost to that member was implied other than a vote in a ballot. The importance of the review ballot success cannot be understated; however, the immediate impact upon depoliticisation was limited, a fact acknowledged by the trade unions in their subsequent response.

IMPLICATIONS OF SUCCESS

The review ballots have brought with them significant implications for trade unionists, specifically, and for politics in general. It would prove useful to analyse those implications under two main headings: (i) the legitimacy of the trade unions involvement in politics; (ii) the reaction of non-fund holders; (iii) the redefinition of trade union political activity; and (iv) aspects of trade union organisation.

The Legitimacy of the Trade Union Political Role

For many active trade unionists defending the right of their union to be involved in the political process was becoming increasingly difficult. Not only was there the concerted questioning by Conservative Government Ministers, as we witnessed during the debates on the 1984 Act, but there was also sound and substantial evidence to indicate that a majority of members both doubted the wisdom of their union's political role, and also failed to vote for the political party to which their union was affiliated. In addition, there was the morale sapping experience of the years of the Thatcher Government which appeared to give credence to the idea that there existed a sharp division between rank-and-file members and trade union leaders, with the one being politically and industrially moderate, whilst the other adopted a more militant political stance.

In response to these criticisms, to a great extent, effective answers were constrained. Although it was possible to talk of the historical nature of trade union political involvement, and of the provisions of the 1913 Act, which allowed for the freedom to opt out of paying the political levy, it was still difficult to conceive of these arguments as an effective defence against the increasing weight of criticism, which was so evident in political controversy, and in the media's coverage and analysis of that controversy. The 1985/6 political fund ballots transformed the whole picture. From being on the defensive, trade union leaders and activists were now able to point to the conclusive evidence of their own ballots. A new legitimacy emerged in two ways.

Firstly, by imposing the requirement of a ballot, the Government created the conditions in which the discussion of politics was both necessary and legitimate. In order to satisfy the Government's wish for a ballot, the unions had been granted, by implication, a necessity to campaign politically. If the ballots were to be the Government's means of curtailing the unions' political role, they possessed, nevertheless, intrinsically the potential of becoming a double edged sword: the threat of defeat co-existed alongside the requirement to campaign politically.

After being told for many years that it was inappropriate for trade unions to become involved in politics, unions were now asked to engage in a ballot which would determine whether they should possess a political role at all.

Hain has noted the paradox in the Government's position:

> Ironically, the Tories may also have done the labour movement something of a backhand long-term favour. By instituting regular political fund ballots they are effectively legitimising political activity and discussion within trade unions, and this could well prove the most lasting consequence of the legislation.

The ballots then, in themselves, offered a legitimacy to the political role. A further stimulus to that legitimacy of course, was provided by the results themselves.

In Chapter 5 it was noted that, in the case of the thirty seven political fund holding unions, twenty achieved an overall majority of support, even when the non-voters were included. Amongst those who voted, the level of support was even more striking, only two unions failed to persuade 70 per cent of those who voted to support the continuation of the union's political role. It is difficult to describe this as other than conclusive support. The need to be defensive disappeared with these ballot results: when union leaders in future engage in the political process they can claim to carry with them the approval of the majority of their members. Maybe for the first time, a real legitimacy could be accorded to the political role. After the 1913 Act, with its distinction between industrial and political activity, there was virtually always a defensive, apologetic aspect to the trade unions' entry into politics. That defensiveness will no longer be appropriate. The 1984 Act, not necessarily by design, gave the unions a new confidence. Without that legislation, as Vine, has commented, 'the biggest and most successful trade union exercise in political education would never have taken place' [3].

The impact of the new legitimacy extends beyond its immediate relevance to the trade unions to the political system itself. It can be argued that the political consensus which emerged in the period after 1945 dealt not only with broad aspects of policy, but also with the institution of politics. Class interests were recognised: capital would be represented through the Conservative Party and industry, labour through its party and the trade unions. Part of the weakening of that consensus could be found in the increasing scepticism about, and opposition to, the link between the Labour Party and the trade unions. The legitimacy flowing from the political fund ballots has reinstated one element of the consensus. This is not to conclude that the overall post-war consensus has suddenly regained its potency. There are too many other aspects of discord and conflict for that to be the case. Nevertheless, the link between the trade unions and the Labour Party which formed a characteristic of that earlier consensus has been given a new strength, permitting possible new political developments, as may already be evidenced by the agreements endorsed by the Labour Party and by the TUC in 1986.

This new legitimacy for the political role has manifested itself in two other ways: by raising the question of whether traditionally non-fund holding unions should ballot their members, and by providing the context in which the fund holders, secure in their substantial majorities, can give systematic thought to their political role.

The Non-Fund Holders

Initially of course, it was the thirty-seven fund holding unions which needed to ballot. As we have seen, the response to that requirement was, in the first place, one of concern about the possible ballot results. However, as success followed success, TUCC was able to react positively, by encouraging non-fund holders to consider holding a ballot. The arguments for such a course of action were straightforward. Firstly, it was suggested, as with other unions, that the new definition of political would severely restrict unions from pursuing their traditional functions: only the positive endorsement of a political fund would lift the potential restrictions. And, secondly, there was a broad recognition that, after the other successes, the climate was right.

The first of the non-fund holding unions to ballot was the National Union of Hosiery and Knitwear Workers (NUHKW). The NUHKW is an interesting case, with its predominantly female, manual worker membership, and its traditions of recruiting industrially and geographically alongside unions which were affiliated to the Labour Party. In many respects, it was difficult to explain why the NUHKW had not agreed to a political fund, and affiliated to the Labour Party many years before. Union officials often explained this phenomenon by reference to the extent to which the Liberal Party had maintained support amongst the working class in areas in which the hosiery industry was well established.

Whether this hypothesis is correct or not, there certainly had been earlier unsuccessful attempts to persuade the membership to support a political fund, with the last occasion having been as recent as 1981. The nature of the 1981 campaign is of intrinsic interest. Consistent with union conference decisions, the NUHKW emphasised not just the value of a political fund, but also the desirability of affiliation to the Labour Party. The date of the ballot was so set as to be able to maximise the anti-Conservative vote. The 1979 Conservative Government was almost halfway through its term of office, suffering the level of unpopularity which is traditionally associated with Governments in mid-term; the County Council elections of May 1981 served to confirm the unpopularity of the Conservative Government. The Union attempted to build upon that, by stressing the benefits of affiliation to the Labour Party, and the ways in which Labour Party policies would work to the advantage of the hosiery industry. The campaign literature reproduced those themes, with prominent articles by the then Labour Party leader, Michael Foot, and by Labour MPs, representing constituencies which included a sizeable hosiery industry interest.

Although the ballot failed to produce a majority for a political fund, with 55 per cent of those voting opposing the idea, the margin of defeat was not substantial, and, as such, it must have provided some optimism as the union contemplated a further ballot in 1986. Following the 1981 ballot, however, the issue appeared to have assumed a low relevance to the union leadership, even though there was a further conference decision asking for another ballot. It was the 1984 Act which provided the opportunity for that ballot to take place.

The style of the 1986 campaign differed markedly from that of 1981: the themes of 1986 were wholly consistent with the TUCC approach, with a strong emphasis upon the right to a voice. It was stressed that the union had a need to engage in political campaigns about, for instance, import controls, and the multi-fibre arrangements, and that the ability to participate in this way would be endangered by the new definition of political under the 1984 Act. This was, then, a familiar approach, with a noticeably lower emphasis upon the prospect of affiliation to the Labour Party, than in the 1981 campaign. For the Hosiery Union leaders, the similarity of their own approach, and that of the TUCC hardly came as a surprise, as they felt that they were influential, based upon their 1981 experience, in helping to shape the TUCC's strategy and thinking.

The emphasis upon the possible constraints on campaigning certainly provoked a strong reaction from the Conservative Government. Although, as we noted in the last chapter, the Government adopted a low profile after the early review ballots, they obviously felt, in relation to the first non-fund holder to ballot, that an intervention might be appropriate. Mr. Kenneth Clarke, the Paymaster General, in drawing attention to what he defined as the issues, again spotlighted the substantial weakness which confronted the Government in clarifying the new statutory definition of political. Clarke commented thus: 'Before they cast their votes members should ask why their own union needs a political fund after so many years without one. The honest answer is that they only need one if they are going to engage in party politics, sponsor a Member of Parliament or finance party election campaigns'. Clarke went on: 'I have no objection to the Knitwear workers voting democratically that they want their union to behave in a party political manner, but I hope that they understand what they are voting for ... The question they need to answer is whether they want their union to spend their money on behalf of a political party' [4].

In what way the Paymaster General's words were heeded is difficult to say, especially as the ballot result, set out in Table 6.3, showed such a decisive majority for establishing a political fund. Support had virtually doubled since 1981, in an election which produced a much larger turnout.

The Paymaster General has accused, by implication, the NUHKW of wishing to fund a political party. Although the union only established its political fund in June 1986, there are no signs, at this admittedly early stage, that the union is taking any immediate steps towards affiliating to the Labour Party. In addition, despite the increase in subscription necessitated by the political fund, there appear to be very few members who have exercised their legal right to opt out.

If the inclusion of the Hosiery Union amongst the numbers holding political funds was of some concern to the Government, there can be no doubt that the next non-fund holding union to ballot, the Inland Revenue Staffs Federation (IRSF) brought acutely to the Government's attention the ironies, and possible imperfections, of the 1984 Act.

Since its election in 1979, the Government had scarcely enjoyed the best of relationships with the Civil Service unions. Almost inevitably, as the Government pursued its commitment to reduce the number of civil servants, it ran into conflict with the unions. In addition to that, there existed a strong feeling in the Civil Service that their pay had been unjustifiably squeezed by the Government. And, finally, there had been the Government's decision of 1984 to ban union membership at the Government Communications Headquarters: that decision had most certainly increased the already noticeable tension between the Government and the Civil Service unions.

Table 6.3: Ballot Results - NUHKW

Ballot papers issued	46,398	
Returned	41,920	(90.3% turnout)
Yes	35,017	
No	6,616	
Spoilt	287	
Majority	28,401	

The decision by the IRSF to hold a political fund ballot must be considered against this background. There was, however, a further twist. The usual understanding of the British constitution is that formally and openly the Civil Service should be neutral. The Government now faced the prospect of its own civil servants, or, at least, a section of them, feeling that they needed to be able to adopt and to finance a political role.

The Government reacted strongly against the possibility of the IRSF holding a ballot, evidently to such an extent that the union had to threaten to pursue legal action in order to gain access to the facilities which they required for the ballot. Furthermore, in a statement in the House of Commons, the Minister of State at the Treasury, Mr. Peter Brooke, repeated the Government's contention that political funds were unnecessary, unless a union wanted to engage in party politics: 'Political funds are unnecessary unless the Civil Service Trade Unions are proposing to participate in party political activities or to campaign for or against political parties or candidates. Provided that this is not the main purpose of their material or activities, they remain free, like other trade unions, to spend money from their general fund to promote and to defend their member's interests. This was the position before the Trade Union Act 1984 came into force and remains the position now' [5].

Added to this general Government contention that nothing had changed, Brooke introduced the extra dimension relating to political neutrality: 'Union members should know also that the creation of such funds will not be seen as in keeping with the political neutrality of a Civil Service that has to serve Governments of any political persuasion'.

In retrospect, it would appear as if the Government's intervention and tactics were counterproductive. The IRSF were able to exploit both the continuing ambiguities of the 1984 Act, and the opposition of their employer. Taken together, these created an atmosphere in which the result, set out in Table 6.4, became almost inevitable.

At the time of writing, a third, smaller union, the Broadcasting Entertainment Trades Alliance (BETA) [6] has

Table 6.4:   Result of Inland Revenue Staffs Federation Ballot

Ballot papers issued	55,751	
Returned	48,734	(87.4% turnout)
Yes	39,776	(81.6% yes)
No	8,872	(18.2% no)
Spoilt papers	86	
Majority	31,904	

joined the NUHKW, and the IRSF, as a previous non-fund-holding union, which has gained membership support for a political fund. It is further suggested that another eleven unions, mainly from the public sector with white collar membership, are likely to hold ballots on the question of political funds. It is in these developments that one can see one of the paradoxes of the 1984 Act.

As we have already commented, thirty-seven trade unions, which were required by the provisions of the legislation to ballot members, have come through that experience without apparent difficulty, and with greater legitimacy accorded to their political role. Whatever its public response, it is difficult to believe that this outcome was ideal as far as the Government was concerned. Indeed, it is a strangely inefficient attack on your opponents defences which leaves your opponent stronger; the first stage of the political fund ballots probably led to that conclusion; the second stage, in which non-fund holders balloted, meant, in reality, that the Government provided reinforcements for their opponents. The double-edged sword of the 1984 Act had worked, without doubt, against the Government's wishes.

Leopold (1986) has adequately described the irony of the Government's position in the following terms:

> The Government had moved the goal posts, so they (i.e. the non-fund holders) needed to fund to stay in the game. Thus the creation of the fund was seen as an insurance policy, lest there be any challenge to spending from general funds on campaigns which could be construed to fall foul of the new definition.

And, he concluded in the following terms about the new definition of political objects:

> The definition of political objects can be seen to have operated to make it easier for unions to campaign for the retention of funds and the establishment of new ones, whereas the original intention was to limit the political campaign activities of the unions.

Trade Union Political Activity

In addition to the ballot results the new confidence in a political role has manifested itself in other ways. Individual unions have given more thought to providing ways of developing coherent political strategies. The impact of those strategies is as yet, impossible to quantify, but the priority which has been accorded to developing political awareness suggests a new earnestness, and a willingness to learn from the previous neglect, which has been described in Chapter 3.

Examples of the new approach are not difficult to find. For instance, Warburton, the principal national officer of the General, Municipal, Boilermakers and Allied Trades Union, claims that his union has responded to the political fund ballot with the following initiatives:

> The GMB has launched a bulletin aimed at officers, Constituency Labour Party delegates and activists. A more frequent and shorter newsbrief has also been launched as well as regular briefings for the union's political officers.

> In every region a political liaison officer has been established, political education and training courses have been introduced in several regions... [7].

In addition to those attempts to enhance the political awareness of their own members, the GMB has initiated a new venture entitled '326 - Labour Target' which strives to link the union much more closely with the Labour Party, especially with those Labour Parties in marginal parliamentary constituencies. The stated objective is to contribute towards the election of a Labour Government.

A similar approach can be seen in the National Union of Railwaymen. According to Knapp, the union's General Secretary, the NUR has been involved in 'three major political initiatives: a joint mailing exercise with the Labour Party, a campaign to promote Labour Party workplace branches, and a new political training programme - all of them aiming to mobilise NUR members in support of the Labour Party in the lead-up to the general election'. As further evidence of both the response, and the confidence, Knapp makes the following comment: 'For us the campaign for a Labour victory will not be a matter of last minute exhortations once the election is announced: the campaign begins now' [8].

These words inferred a different approach from hitherto: instead of taking their own members' political support for granted, the union appeared to recognise a long-term need to campaign on political issues. Whilst the results of this different approach will take some time to come through, and may be always difficult to quantify, there may already be signs that the political fund campaigns are producing certain dividends.

A number of unions have already indicated increases in the number of members paying the political levy. GMB, COHSE and ACTT for instance, fall into that category; as evidently, do ASTMS. The ASTMS example is of particular interest, as this is a union is which political levy paying has been very much a minority pursuit. Following the declaration of its ballot result, the union, through its Journal, sent out a card, signed by the General Secretary, inviting members to pay the levy. It would appear as if that approach has resulted in an increase in levy payers.

Even if the increase in each individual union is small, the significance cannot be overstated, because, unlike the usual processes, members are being asked to take the positive step of agreeing to contribute to the political funds. Normally, of course, the active step is in the direction of opting-out. In this context, of further significance is the fact that it is those members who have previously decided to opt out, who are now notifying their union of their wish to contribute. Again, this would appear to be an initially unexpected consequence of the review ballots.

The picture, then, emerges of individual unions developing a coherent approach to their political role, subsequent to and consequent upon the review ballots. An additional development concerns the decision to act collectively, through the formation of Trade Unionists for Labour (TUFL).

During the period of the review ballots, two separate organisations existed: TUCC with specific objectives in terms of the ballot, and, continuing to exist alongside it, Trade Unionists for a Labour Victory, (TULV) with its broader remit. It became increasingly apparent that there would be value in trying to build up the campaigning successes of TUCC, and to translate these into the post review ballot era. For this reason, a joint meeting of TUCC and TULV was held in December 1985, with the purpose of looking for an effective long-term merger of the two organisations. A working party was established and it reported to a further joint meeting, held in February 1986, attended not just by representatives of TULV and TUCC, but also by the Labour Party Leader, and the Party's General Secretary. It was this meeting which gave birth to TUFL with the consequent decision to wind up both TUCC and TULV.

In opening the meeting, the Chairman, Mr. Ron Todd, the General Secretary of the Transport and General Workers Union, drew specific attention to two guiding principles set out in the working party's report. They were:

(i) that under no circumstances whatsoever would the new organisation concern itself with matters of party policy; and

(ii) that if any union felt that it wanted to be associated only with the organisational aspect - and not with the financial arrangements - it would be entitled to do so [9].

In setting out these two principles there can be little doubt that certain conclusions had been drawn from the previous experience of TULV. The financial arrangements, by allowing a substantial degree of freedom, would equally

encourage the broadest possible membership. More importantly, though, by stating its resolve not to become involved
in aspects of party policy, it was anticipated that TUFL might
avoid the criticism experienced by TULV, in that for many,
TULV was too closely involved in sectional conflicts within the
Party. The working party report was explicit on this point:

> Policy decisions of the Party are for them alone, be it
> through Annual Conference, NEC or PLP. The trade
> union policy influence can legitimately be exercised
> through the TUC-LP Liaison Committee. It has to be said
> quite emphatically that whilst any new structure must
> organise in total co-operation with the Party, come what
> may, policy decisions are for the Party alone [10].

After excluding policy considerations, certain aims were
attributed to TUFL. In the preamble to the objectives, the
main goal is described as the return and maintenance in
power of a Labour Government. Four aims and objectives were
then set out in the constitution of TUFL:

> a) To maintain and exploit the impetus provided by the
> political fund ballots campaign by increasing political
> awareness amongst trade unionists and strengthening the
> political links between the unions and the Labour Party
> at all levels in a co-ordinated form.

> b) To increase membership of the Labour Party and levy
> paying members to union political funds.

> c) By close co-operation with the Party to maximise
> assistance that trade unionists give to all levels of the
> Party, and

> d) To constitute regional committees which would
> implement agreed decisions of the all trade unions com-
> mittee and/or the Executive Committee [11].

The influence of TUCC is quickly discerned: like the
review campaigns, TUFL would be charged with the responsibility of persuading individual trade unionists to respond.
Again, the emphasis will be upon the workplace, building
upon the notion of having secured the trade union political
voice. Response can be elicited at a number of levels: by
persuading those who currently opt out of the political levy
to consider paying in the future; by persuading more
members to join the Labour Party, and to play an active part;
and, at an organisational level, creating the conditions in
which more trade union branches affiliate to local Constituency Labour Parties. In addition, TUFL is expected to contribute towards the Labour Party's own campaigns: by

improving the electoral organisation in those target constituencies which the Labour Party must win in order to form
a government; and, by playing a part in those Labour Party
campaign initiatives which are designed to draw attention to
specific issues or themes.

The organisational shape of TUFL is broadly similar to
that of TUCC. There will be a general committee - an all
Trades Union Committee, which will meet every two months,
and which will involve possible participation by all unions
affiliated to the Labour Party, plus the Labour Party's
General Secretary. Additionally, it was agreed that an
executive committee of twelve would be elected annually, and
that it would meet on a monthly basis to oversee the attain-
ment of agreed objectives. It is interesting to note that the
working party's report originally suggested an executive of
ten, but that this was broadened to twelve at the inaugural
meeting when it was found that twelve nominations had been
received for the ten places; maybe an indication of the
priority which was attached to maintaining consensus and
unity.

Again, as with TULV and TUCC, TUFL is to possess its
own regional tiers, involving local full-time union officers and
regional officials of the Labour Party; and its own national
unit, comprised of Bill Keys as the National Campaign Co-
ordinator, with two other full-time members of staff.

At the time of writing, TUFL's life has been no more
than a few months. There are, however, early indications of
involvement in local government elections, in Labour Party
campaigns, and, maybe most importantly, in trying to
persuade individual trade unionists to become both more
supportive to the Labour Party, and more active in its
affairs. It is in this context that the influence of the review
ballots is most noticeable. The unions have gained the confidence and the legitimacy to campaign for their party
amongst their own members. Furthermore, they have developed understanding and techniques which lead them to believe
that they can make positive contact with their members.
TUFL, it would seem, is not designed as an organisation
which will provide the Labour Party with a financial drip
feed; or which will come to life at general elections in the,
judging from past experience, forlorn hope of suddenly
persuading their members to vote Labour. TUFL is regarded
as an organisation which will campaign amongst rank-and-file
trade unionists for the labour case before, during and beyond
the next general election. These aims, and the very existence
of TUFL indicate, yet again, the irony of the 1984 Act. It
was that legislation which made TUFL and its approach
possible.

EXPLANATIONS AND IMPLICATIONS

ASPECTS OF TRADE UNION ORGANISATION

As is so often the case, the review ballots brought with them
certain unexpected benefits; in this particular context, these
benefits have occurred in relation to trade union organisation.

The rules for the conduct of the ballots, as set out by
the 1913 Act, and as interpreted by the Certification Officer,
insist that each individual member should enjoy an equal
right, and, if possible, a fair opportunity of voting, in
conditions where the secrecy of the ballot is assured. Whilst
the 1913 Act provision was supplemented by the 1984 Act, the
most significant change was one of atmosphere brought about
by the provisions of Part I of the 1984 Act. Those provisions
relate only to the conduct of elections for the unions' principal executive committee. They are, however, so drafted that
they make it virtually impossible for a union to administer
those elections by other than either a postal ballot, or a
mixture of postal and workplace ballot. This new requirement
meant that individual unions were giving particular attention
to the rule changes necessary to bring their election procedures into line with the criteria set out in the 1984 Act.

It is therefore scarcely surprising that the model which
was being developed for executive elections should be applied
by the unions themselves to the political fund ballots. A
further provision of the 1984 Act also assumed some relevance. In the final stages of the passage of the 1984 Act,
the Government introduced a new clause imposing an obligation upon trade unions to compile a register of their
members. Whilst the unions objected to this duty, as they did
with even more vigour to the conditions laid down for the
conduct of elections to the principal executive committee, in
retrospect a certain benefit may well have accrued.

Most unions have traditionally not been in the position to
provide an accurate list of their membership. There are many
reasons for this: the changing composition of membership, the
dependence upon lay activists whose bureaucratic skills vary
considerably, the failure of employers handling members
subscriptions on a check-off system to notify the union of
changes when they take place, and, in some cases, the
secrecy of membership. All of these factors contributed to the
inaccuracy of union membership records.

The political fund ballots necessitated a new accuracy,
and a concern for detail. With this in mind, all the unions
devoted a good deal of time, and resources, in the period
preceding their ballot, to compiling an up-to-date electoral
register. This, incidentally, applied not just to those unions
who were required to conduct a review ballot; it was equally
relevant to non-fund holding unions. In a paper reviewing
their political fund ballot which was submitted to the Hosiery
Union's 1986 Conference, it was simply noted that 'the first

necessity in organising the ballot was to draw up an electoral register of all members of the union' [12].

There can be little doubt that the process of drawing up a register was of organisational value to unions. Almost for the first time, they could identify with some confidence their members. The opposite of that was equally true: non-members could also be identified. A number of unions have claimed that this process, coupled with the activity of the political fund campaigns created the opportunity for extending union membership. There is a view, in NUPE, for instance, that, after a relatively quiescent period, the combined impact of the campaign with its emphasis upon workplace activity, plus the newly reinforced knowledge about gaps in membership, helped to stimulate new recruitment. The Hosiery Union came to a similar conclusion:

> The interest created in the factories by the consultation and information process generated discussion about trade unions, and in many cases this did result in members joining the union. Another factor which led to new members joining the union was that compiling the register of members and issuing that register to union representatives enabled those representatives to identify the people not in the union.

> This process is often difficult with the check-off system. It was found that potential members had just been missed and had never been approached to join the union. Where they were identified and approached, there was often no problem in them taking up union membership [13].

There is a further organisational spin-off. For many unions, the ballot campaigns enabled them to develop an effective workplace network of contacts and activists. In many respects, this may prove to be the most valuable gain, especially taking note of what had happened during the recent years of recession. As redundancies had taken place, it was often the union activists who found themselves on the list of those to lose their jobs. In many workplaces, this meant that union organisation had been effectively deprived of its key activists, and also of the main point of contact between the union at the place of work, and the union outside. This represents a severe weakness, exacerbated as it is by the more aggressive managerial styles which have developed along with high levels of unemployment, and which, often, have imposed a high premium upon the role of lay union activists. Whilst the political fund campaigns have not in themselves transformed this position, they have enabled unions, often in a less aggressive atmosphere, to re-build previous workplace networks.

EXPLANATIONS AND IMPLICATIONS

All of these benefits in organisational terms cannot equal
the unquantifiable but crucially important new confidence
which has flown from the ballot results. We have already
commented upon what that means for the union's political role;
but the confidence also extends to other aspects of organisation. For a number of years, unions had not been just
subject to political criticism, they had also seen their
organisation's vitality drain away under the pressure of the
recession and government policy. The stage had almost been
reached where key figures in the trade unions had come to
doubt their ability to gain membership support for particular
course of action. The political fund campaigns demonstrated
that all was not necessarily gloom; and the conclusion could
easily be drawn that, if it was possible to organise effectively
around the union's political role, surely it was possible to
repeat that success on other issues.

SUMMARY

This chapter has drawn attention to the way in which the
trade unions, through their umbrella organisation, the TUCC,
skillfully defined the agenda of the political fund campaigns,
so as to strike a deep resonance amongst their members. That
reflected itself not simply in the ballot results, but in the
more significant confidence and legitimacy which the unions
were able to attribute to their political role. In turn, that will
manifest itself in a new open and aggressive style through
which the unions aim to achieve a greater political awareness,
operating at all levels from an increase in the numbers paying
the political levy to campaigns for the return of a Labour
Government. As a result of the 1984 Act, union politics are
alive and well, and are being organised so as to influence the
general body of political activity; quite the opposite from
what the unions feared might happen as they embarked upon
the ballot campaigns.

NOTES

1. 'British Public Opinion', a Newsletter reviewing the
results of polls conducted by Market and Opinion Research
International (MORI).
2. Bruce Spencer, 'Trade Unions' Political Funds', un-
published, The Department of Adult and Continuing Education, University of Leads, 1986.
3. Steve Vine, 'Bite the Ballot', New Socialist,
September 1985.
4. Kenneth Clarke, Department of Employment, Press
Notice, January 29th, 1986.
5. Peter Brooke, Hansard, 7th February 1986, Col. 571.

6. The result in the BETA ballot was follows:

Ballot Papers Issued	37,107	
Returned	11,073	(29.84% turnout)
Yes	7,961	(71.89% Yes)
No	3,083	(28.11% No)
Spoilt	29	
Majority	4,878	

7. D. Warburton, 'GMB for Labour Campaign launched to follow up levy ballot' Tribune 30th May, 1986.

8. J. Knapp, 'The NUR launches a major new political initiative'. Tribune 28th March, 1986.

9. Report of a Joint Meeting of TULV and TUCC held in The Boardroom, Transport House, Smith Square, London SW1, on February 25th, 1986, p. 2.

10. Quoted from 'Organising for Labour' - a working group paper.

11. Quoted from Constitution of Trade Unionists for Labour.

12. Quoted from Political Fund Ballot Report, tabled at the 1986 Conference of the National Union of Hosiery and Knitwear Workers.

13. Quoted from Political Fund Ballot Report.

Chapter Seven

FUTURE DEVELOPMENTS

The success, from the unions' viewpoint, of the political fund ballots has helped to shape and to develop a new agenda. Three dominant themes have emerged either directly or indirectly: the nature of political party funding, the role of trade unions within the Labour Party, and the scope for ballots as a means of determining members' opinion. This chapter aims to discuss these issues.

POLITICAL PARTY FUNDING

Whatever the Government's formal justification might have been for the review ballots, the cutting edge of the rhetoric of Government supporters concentrated upon the alleged control exerted by trade union leaders over the policies of the Labour Party. Through the purse strings, so the argument continued, the unions could dominate a Labour Government. For many, the review ballots would offer the opportunity of undermining that potential dominance; for others, as we saw, for instance, with Townend in the House of Commons debates, it was hoped that a Labour Party, stripped of trade union funds, would give way to the Social Democratic Party, as the main opponents of the Conservative Party, thereby creating a party political system in which principled support for the basic notions of capitalism was never questioned. All these hopes and expectations have failed to materialise, leaving behind, as we have already noted, a new and virile legitimacy for the trade unions in their political role. This development provides the trade unions, and the Labour Party, with the chance to discuss political funding from the advantageous position which they currently enjoy as a result of the review ballots.

Before looking at the options open in relation to funding, it might be worthwhile to remind ourselves of the present arrangements. As the two main parties, the Conservative and Labour Parties rely to a considerable extent upon institutional finance, either through companies in the one case or the trade unions in the other. All the minority parties, in contrast, exist almost wholly on monies raised through individual subscriptions and fund raising, with the partial exception of the Liberal Party and the Social Democratic Party which have received limited financial support from certain companies. In addition to these basic sources, each of the parties with representation in Parliament receives public money in order to enable them to carry out their parliamentary duties. The figures for 1985 are set out in Table 7.1.

We possess, then, a hybrid system of political funding, with elements of institutional, private and state finance. The two main areas of debate and controversy have been concerned with the rules for, and the extent of, institutional finance: and with the extent to which state funding can offer an advisable and worthwhile alternative.

As far as institutional finance is concerned, attention has focused upon the different ground rules which apply, in the one case, for trade union contributions to the Labour Party, and, in the other, company donations to the Conservative Party. These differences are stark, and, therefore, easy to summarise: unlike companies, trade unions are bound by special provisions which define and constrain their political role; which create the duty, before assuming any such political role, for the unions to establish a separate fund, which must be approved in a ballot by their members, and, now, as a result of the 1984 Act, affirmed in a regular review ballot; and which allow individual members to opt out of paying to the political fund. None of these requirements applies to companies who are merely obliged to report donations above a certain amount in their annual company accounts.

Table 7.1: Amount Paid to Opposition Parties in 1985 under the scheme whereby provision is made for financial assistance to Opposition Parties in carrying out their Parliamentary duties

Labour Party	£440,355
Liberal Party	88,641
Social Democratic Party	62,562
Ulster Unionist Party	19,889
Scottish National Party	7,977
Democratic Unionist Party	6,789
Plaid Cymru	4,878

Source: Parliamentary Written Answer June 23rd, 1986

The possible response to these disparities can assume two forms: either one argues for an approach which places companies on the same footing as trade unions; or, the other way round, trade unions on the same basis as companies. There are superficial attractions in arguing that companies should be treated in exactly the same way as trade unions: if companies want to extend beyond their primary role, which can be broadly defined as aiming to provide goods and services at a profit, there is some immediate equity in the notion that they should be treated in an identical way to trade unions. There is, in addition, not just an argument based upon parity of treatment; there is equally forcefully a case to be made out on democratic grounds. Shareholders invest money in companies, presumably in order to achieve an income from their capital; workers invest their labour in order to earn a wage, and, to enjoy a degree of job security; there is no manifest evidence, in either case, that they might wish that part of the wealth which they help to create, in their different ways, should be spent on supporting, in the main, the Conservative Party. This is an argument which has never been effectively countered by Conservative politicians, especially as the logic of the argument runs inexorably towards arrangements whereby company shareholders, and, possibly, employees would be asked either on a once and for all basis, or regularly, to sanction the use of company monies for political purposes. The case, then, for imposing upon companies similar requirements as those currently in force for trade unions must be an attractive option for trade unionists, especially as such a course could be justified both in terms of equity, and of democracy.

It could further be argued that such arrangements would also be beneficial to consumers. Given that many major companies, producers of well known consumer goods, feel that it is in their interests to contribute to the Conservative Party, it must be reasonable to conclude that many purchases, which contribute admittedly in a very limited amount to Conservative Party funds, are made by individuals who do not support that party. If one accepts the principle of informed participation in politics, then this practice is not easy to defend. Without advocating a system of opting-out for consumers, it could be suggested that the introduction of effective democratic accountability over company contributions will ensure that the public, hence the consumer, is better informed.

The alternative approach would involve imposing the same rights and duties upon trade unions as currently obtain for companies. The attraction of this approach can be regarded as substantial, for one over-riding reason. Since the judgement in the Osborne case and the subsequent legislative response in the 1913 Trade Union Act, a debilitating differentiation has been introduced into trade union activities:

those matters, which are deemed industrial, are considered to be mainstream, and treated under one set of rules, whilst political matters are thrust to the margins, and treated in a more restricted and restricting manner. Certain significant consequences flow from this.

The natural fusion and overlap between the industrial and the political are blurred, to the disadvantage of the unions. It is still very much the case that government decisions either directly or indirectly affect the life chances of trade union members; hence, the clear political dimension. However, by imposing a distinction between the two types of activity, the natural flow from the political to the industrial, and vice versa, is prevented. This process has resulted in the unions being placed on the defensive about their political role, often leading, as we saw in Chapter 3, to a damaging neglect of the need to discuss and organise around political issues. For these reasons it could be argued that it would be beneficial for the trade unions to campaign for a return to what was regarded as the legal position, prior to the Osborne case.

As one might anticipate, there are, however, voices raised against this possible approach, not least amongst trade unionists. There are, for instance, those who have become attracted to the notion of regular review ballots, partly, it might be suggested, as a result of the euphoria surrounding the first successful round of ballots. From this standpoint, the benefits of regular ballots are stressed, notably that process of concentrating the mind, which forced politics on to the trade union agenda, and created the stimulant for what have undeniably been effective campaigns. Regular ballots, it is argued, would ensure that unions need to give thought to their political role, and to those means by which they can secure the acquiescence and the support of their members for that. In short, periodic ballots would create the requirement for continuing political education. There are merits in this argument, not least in the willingness to try to mould Conservative legislation to the benefit of the trade unions. Some caution and scepticism may, however, not be totally inappropriate. To suggest that the first round success in the review ballots can be repeated on subsequent occasions may be much too optimistic, especially if one takes account of the favourable timing, coinciding as it did with a relatively unpopular Conservative Government. It is not difficult to envisage the unions facing substantial problems in gaining majority support, if future ballots were to coincide not with an unpopular phase of Conservative Government, but with a similar period in the life of a Labour administration. Furthermore, one suspects that once the members have rejected a political fund for their union, it might be more difficult to generate sufficient enthusiasm in the future for the re-establishment of the political fund. Therefore, realistically, it has to be admitted that regular ballots represent a risky strategy. The question which the trade unions will need to answer is whether they consider that risk worthwhile. For some, it certainly would be, not least for the opportunity which it offers to organise a political campaign. There is, however, in this notion a certain degree of defeatism or cynicism: implied is a conclusion that without the statutory requirement, the trade unions will once more relegate their political role to a low priority.

There is an additional source of doubt amongst trade unionists about the proposal to put trade union funding on the same basis as companies. There is a not insubstantial fear that many trade union members would object to part of their contribution being used to finance the Labour Party [1]. The evidence to substantiate this fear is somethat contradictory: in general terms, only a small percentage of trade union members exercise their right to opt out, although, as we have already noted, a much larger percentage, even constituting a majority in 1983, have voted other than Labour in elections. Maybe this latter figure is irrelevant, as one of the effective arguments in the review campaigns centred upon persuading members that the political fund is required for purposes other than supporting the Labour Party; the minority, who have decided to opt out, cannot however be considered as irrelevant. If they currently object to paying the political levy, would those objections, in the context in which there was only one membership contribution with no provision for a political levy, be subsequently transferred to the question of union membership itself? In these circumstances, a judgement would have to be made on the number of members likely to be lost; but, more importantly, the unions would have to decide whether they consider it desirable and feasible to argue for the removal of a right which has been enjoyed by a small minority of trade unionists since 1913.

This, and other issues, indicate the fluid state of the debate on political funding. By their success in the review ballots, the unions find themselves in a powerful position to shape the agenda of that debate, but, before that, certain questions need to be answered:

(a) What approach will the unions be adopting towards the rules for company political donations?

(b) How strong is the argument for removing the restrictions on the unions' political role, so that funding by unions should be on the same basis as companies. If that approach is adopted, how is it possible to safeguard the rights of the small minority who currently opt out of the political levy? A possible solution in this respect might be found in identifying an element of contribution, which could be considered as the political payment, and out of which a member could opt; whilst, at the same time, the total membership contribution would go to one fund which could then be used for all purposes, be they industrial or political. This compromise appears to have the advantage of protecting the minority, whilst largely avoiding the false distinction between industrial and political.

(c) And if the broad framework of the 1913 Act is to be restored, what attitude will be taken to the 1984 provision for regular balloting? Incidentally, it must be pointed out the rights of the minority in relation to opting out of the political levy are neither positively nor negatively affected by the need for regular ballots. All regular ballots provide is the opportunity to decide whether the union should have a political fund, not whether an individual can opt out of contributing to that fund.

Although not immediately related to the principles of funding, the question of opting-out or opting-in has provided a consistent thread, running through all the debates since 1913. The review ballots may well serve to quieten that debate for some time. An opportunity has been provided for union members to express their wishes about the continued existence of a political fund for their union. Not only has there been an overwhelming expression of support, but, in certain unions, the numbers voting 'no' were substantially smaller than those opting out of the levy payment. Two comments, then, become appropriate. Firstly, there can be little doubt that many, who have exercised their right to opt out of paying the political levy, must have cast their vote in favour of maintaining the political fund. And, secondly, given the overwhelming support for political funds, it is difficult to assert that there are considerable numbers of trade unionists keen to dissociate themselves from the political fund, but prevented from doing so. The regular allegations of intimidation are not going to be easy to sustain given the experience of the review ballots; that experience, regardless of whatever conclusions are reached on the more general issues of funding, coupled with the TUC guidance on opting-out provisions, must surely ensure that the possibility of introducing opting-in is unlikely to make any meaningful political progress in the forseeable future.

For some, however, the practice of institutional and corporate funding is unacceptable, in so far as it guarantees to capital and labour, influence over one or other of the main political parties. That guarantee is seen as underpinning a political system, which emphasises conflict, and class differences, at the cost of consensus, and, ultimately, of economic performance. Taken with other constitutional changes, such

107

as the introduction of some system of proportional representation, it is argued that the reformation of political parties outside the institutions of class conflict would contribute to improved economic management. Public or state funding of those parties provides an essential component of this package of reform.

To some extent, in recent years, the arguments about state funding have taken place on a false assumption. There is, as we have seen, already state funding of political parties. The question, therefore, mainly shifts from one of principle to one of degree. The review ballots may well have ensured that the current balance is broadly maintained. By voting for the continuation of the political funds, union members can be regarded, by inference, as acquiescing in the existing patterns of financial support in general, and in the level of support offered by individual trade unions to the Labour Party. Making the same point negatively, it is now going to be difficult to sustain an effective case against trade union funding of the Labour Party. And, even more prosaically, given that the Labour Party can now look forward to trade union financial support, the Labour Party is hardly likely to throw itself into a campaign to extend significantly the scope of state financing.

Apart from the somewhat cynical lack of immediate need, there may be other valid reasons as to why the Labour Party should not wish to change drastically the balance between institutional and state funding. Alongside anxieties about the possible risk of too close a link between state and political party, there are also grounds for concern about changing the nature of the Labour Party. If, as so often is claimed, the unique strength of the Labour Party is to be found in the potential which is derived from the unions' financial and organisational resources, and which, in turn, provide the opportunity through which it is possible to secure and to sustain political support amongst at least, those sections of the working class which are organised into trade unions, changing and devaluing that relationship may well transform the essential nature of the Labour Party. In Chapter 4, it was suggested that life without the trade unions may not offer an attractive prospect for the Labour Party; that viewpoint was expressed in the context of possible defeats in the review ballots, but the same sentiments could equally apply to changes brought about by a greater dependence upon state funding. Not least in importance amongst those changes would be the possible shift in power from Party conference to the Parliamentary Party. As more money from the public purse flowed into the party, and, almost inevitably for organisational reasons, into a combination of Party Head Office and the Parliamentary Party, a new centre of influence, and of policy making, would be consolidated. The resultant loss in influence would be felt by the Constituency Labour Parties, and by the trade unions. For those reasons, it appears difficult to anticipate any enthusiasm from the unions for a greater dependence by political parties upon state funding: it is much more probable that the unions will concentrate upon the issues already referred to. In other words, the debate is likely to be mainly concerned with the principles and details of institutional and corporate funding.

TRADE UNIONS WITHIN THE LABOUR PARTY

The review ballots have endorsed the trade unions' political role, and, by extension, their involvement in the Labour Party. That endorsement was achieved after campaigns in each union which succeeded in stimulating a much higher degree of participation than has been true in relation to so many union activities. The question which emerges is whether, following that success, the unions can find processes through which they can enhance the extent of involvement in those decisions affecting the Labour Party.

Decision making in the Labour Party depends upon indirect democracy, whereby delegates cast votes on behalf of the union membership, and in accordance with policy determined through the unions' own internal structures. Necessarily, everyone favours greater participation by union members, but differences exist as to the most efficient means of turning that aspiration into an objective.

We have already seen that certain unions and TUFL are devoting resources to persuade individual members to play a greater part in the Labour Party. The emphasis is upon persuading more trade unionists to become individual members of the Labour Party, and upon urging local branches to affiliate to the appropriate Constituency Labour Party. If successful, all of this will enhance the prospect of providing for a wider and better informed participation. Serious problems, however, remain to be resolved.

In many unions, geographical branches provide the base of the organisational pyramid. It is in those branches very often that political resolutions are first discussed; and, it is in those branches that attendance is at a very low level.

Without for a moment trying to detract from the contribution to the union's well-being made by those who attend branch meetings, it is difficult not to recognise the potentially unrepresentative character of a decision which might have been taken by no more than one or two per cent of the membership. The contrast which is valid and relevant is not merely with the participation rates in the review ballots, but, with the generally greater involvement experienced in workplace union branches. This contrast raises, of course, many fundamental concerns, not least a recognition that the pattern of trade union organisation considered appropriate in the early days of trade unionism, might now be inappropriate for a changed membership, and for different employment conditions. The archetypal branch meeting, held in the evening in a city centre public house, often seems designed for those days when male manual work dominated the economy. In order to attract more women members, part-time workers and those from the new technology and service industries, it is essential to question deeply the current organisation of trade union affairs. Whilst a good deal of attention has been devoted to the role of the law in providing conditions for greater internal democracy, one is often left with the impression that more could have been achieved if a similar interest had been shown in developing more effective systems or organisation. No readily available panacea exists: whilst workplace branches might offer an attractive route for some unions, or even for parts of unions, there will be substantial sections of membership who cannot be organised into workplace branches. These issues will, however, have to be faced if the unions are to foster conditions in which the members will participate more in decision making, be it on industrial or political matters.

Indirect democracy depends not just upon the initial level of involvement but also upon the extent to which those who represent others clearly act on behalf of others; accountability is a necessary condition for effective indirect democracy. At national level, the processes of accountability appear to work satisfactorily: union policy has mostly already been determined, and is often widely known. In the majority of instances, union delegations to the Labour Party Conference will be bound by existing policies, although freedom, and, maybe licence often prevail in relating a union's policy to the specific motions to be discussed at conference. It is at local level, however, where local union branches send delegates to Constituency Labour Parties that doubt frequently arises as to the degree of accountability. Sometimes the reasons for these doubts may be found in the limited scope of branch meetings: or in the need for delegates to respond immediately to issues being discussed at constituency party meetings. In addition, however, there are examples of union branch affiliations being used, in a rotten borough manner, as a means of maximising sectional support, be it of the right or of the left, on the Management Committee of a Constituency Party.

If individual unions and the TUFL are going to encourage greater affiliation to local labour parties, then the nature of the indirect democracy working at that level needs to be examined. Given that the local level provides individual union members very often with their only experience of trade union involvement in the Labour Party, it is even more essential that the mechanisms of accountability should be seen to work efficiently.

Even though the general argument is always for enhanced membership involvement, one senses, ironically, that one particular cause adopted by certain trade unions, in the name of democracy, may work in a different way in practice. Under existing arrangements, prospective Labour candidates, including those in constituencies already represented by a Labour MP, are selected by a general committee, comprising delegates from local Labour Party branches and from local trade union branches. This pattern reflects the usual procedures for delegated democracy in the Labour Party. There are those who would prefer to see this system substantially revised, by shifting the decision from the General Committee to a ballot of each individual member [2]. It is argued that, through this method, what is regarded as the most important and sensitive decision taken by the local party, would be more democratic, as it is open to all individual members.

At one level this is an attractive proposition, but care is required to ensure that, if this change takes place, other consequences detrimental to the trade unions do not follow. For instance, by defining the electorate as paid-up Labour Party members, one is excluding all those affiliated trade unionists who might wish to express a preference through their trade union procedures. In addition, by specifically arguing that one decision is of such crucial importance that it must be taken outside the normal processes, doubt is being cast upon the appropriateness and the efficacy of those procedures in other contexts. If in some sense they are deficient in one context, it may be possible to argue that similar deficiencies prevail in relation to other decisions. By sustaining that argument, it is possible to transform the traditional decision making of the party, thereby reducing the input of the trade unions.

Whatever the outcome of the debate about selection procedures for prospective parliamentary Labour candidates, the broader question of the means by which it might prove possible to enhance the level of involvement by individual trade union members in the affairs of the Labour Party will remain. The review ballots have ensured the safety of the bones; it is now the responsibility of trade unions to seek means of putting flesh upon those bones.

THE USE OF BALLOTS

The 1984 Trade Union Act imposed a statutory duty either to hold ballots of the membership, or to conduct ballots in a specified manner. In many cases, unions had previously conducted ballots on the issues covered by the Act. We have already seen the provision in relation to political funds.

The 1984 Act extended also to the conduct of elections for a union's principal executive committee; and to industrial

111

action, if a union was to continue to enjoy the legal immunities derived originally from the 1906 Act, but subsequently
heavily restricted by the 1980, and the 1982 Employment
Acts.

Before looking at the controversy stimulated by these
provisions, it might be worthwhile just examining the limited
experience of the 1984 Act. As for political fund ballots, the
outcome is known, and the trade unions could hardly have
been more successful. In relation to industrial action, the
Advisory, Conciliation and Arbitration Service's (ACAS)
annual report for 1985 provides the most extensive information.

At the end of the year the Service had become aware of
94 cases in which ballots had been organised, involving
no fewer than 37 trade unions. Of these 68 resulted in a
majority vote for industrial action and 25 against with
one tie. In 38 of the cases where voting was in favour
of action stoppages or other industrial action took place
and 23 resulted in no action. It is not clear whether all
ballots held complied with the strict terms of the Act. In
15 cases we were aware that injunctions had been sought
by employers in the courts, either because no ballot had
taken place before industrial action began, or because
they considered that ballots which had been held did not
meet all the requirements of the Act [3].

From those ACAS figures, it can be concluded that
industrial action ballots had not, in themselves, been particularly damaging to trade unions. In over 70 per cent of the
cases, members had supported industrial action. In addition,
it is worth noting that ballots had taken place in no more
than 12 per cent of reported disputes: in 1985, there were
813 officially recorded stoppages, but only 94 ballots. The
provisions of the 1984 Act had not become all consuming in
practice.

The experience of the balloting requirements of the 1984
Act may not have been as difficult as many trade unionists
feared. Nevertheless, that experience could not in itself meet
the traditional viewpoint that internal affairs of a union were
of concern to members alone; the state had no right to interfere. The problem facing the trade unions, during 1985 and
1986, was how to respond to the experience of ballots, and
how to square that response with the principled viewpoint of
opposition to state involvement. That problem in turn gave
rise to another: what role would the law play in future
organisation of industrial relations, and of trade unions?

Taking the latter question first, the unions were
conscious of how the law had traditionally granted immunity
and not rights. Experience had shown, from the unions'
viewpoint, the dangers and weaknesses of immunities; unions

had always been subject to the criticism that they were above the law, in that, whilst their actions might be illegal at common law, the immunities granted enabled them to be free from legal action. Furthermore, the scope of immunities was necessarily fluid, and, therefore, subject to restrictive judicial interpretation. From the early 1960s onwards, the judges appeared to have used every opportunity to restrict trade union action; the case of Rookes v Barnard [4] was the precursor of many others. Whilst there were doubts about the value of immunities, no such hesitation existed as far as the legislation enacted from 1979 onwards was concerned. That was to be repealed. That statement, of course, made it even more imperative that there should be some form of broad agreement on the contribution which the law might make in industrial relations.

Some immediate resolution can be found in the TUC-Labour Party document People at Work: New Rights, New Responsibilities, which was endorsed by the TUC conference in 1986, and which aims to set out principles for the role of the law. According to the document, the law 'can be given a positive role - with new rights and protection for individual workers and their unions' [5].

Individual rights are seen as underpinning collective rights and collective bargaining; there is no tension, as such, between the two. This position is contrasted with that of the current government who are accused of using 'the language of individual rights to attack collective rights and the ability of trade unions to defend their members' [6]. The Labour Party and the TUC would endeavour, in contrast, 'to take steps to promote trade union membership and organisation; to encourage union recognition by employers for collective bargaining purposes; and to develop and support stable and effective negotiating machinery' [7].

Not only would the processes of collective bargaining be encouraged, but so would the scope. The objective is to extend the collective bargaining agenda beyond the traditional topics of wages and conditions. In this way, progress towards greater industrial democracy could be achieved, with collective bargaining offering the means of achieving that aim. Collectively, workers are to be given the opportunity of becoming more involved in decision making at company level, and in sector and national planning. For the TUC and the Labour Party, it is axiomatic that 'those who are affected by change must be able to have a far greater control over the nature and direction of change' [8].

Implied in the collective bargaining process is the ability to impose sanctions; in the case of workers, the ability to take some form of industrial action. It is, at this point, that the new notion of providing positive law, which, in any case, will be subject to judicial interpretation, comes face to face with the thorny question of immunities. The TUC-Labour

Party statement claims that it is 'vital that the law guarantees the essential legal freedom of workers and their unions to organise effective industrial action, without the continued threat of employers launching debilitating legal actions against employees' [9]. The question remains, however, of how this is to be achieved.

Immunities, and the basis of the law since 1906, provide the answer. The new approach, it is suggested, will incorporate a mixture of rights, immunities and responsibilities. The protection given by immunities, now substantially restricted by the 1980 and 1982 Employment Acts, will be redefined and broadened. The notion of a legal right to strike is still rejected in favour of immunities.

In addition to extending collective rights, the new positive law would be used to offer greater protection to individual employees. To a great extent, this is a reproduction of the philosophy behind the 1975 Employment Protection Act. That legislation, which also established rights for individuals, was based to a certain extent upon the limitations of collective bargaining. If those limitations were present in the mid-1970s, they are much more obvious and stark in the mid-1980s, in the context of high unemployment, reduced unionisation and new patterns of employment. For Edmonds, the General Secretary of GMBATU, the new employment rights would represent the trade unions coming to the rescue of the 'throwaway people in a throwaway economy' [10]. The new servant class would derive some protection from exploitation as a result of the measures which the document proposed.

If the law was to play a positive role, extending and linking collective and individual rights, the question about the use of ballots remained. The option of simply repealing the 1980 and 1982 Acts was still valid and it attracted support within the trade unions. For some, it was necessary to remind fellow trade unionists that ballots for a range of decisions had always taken place, and that, if there was pressure to extend the scope of balloting, unions rule books were sufficiently flexible to allow this to take place. The state was, at best, irrelevant; but the state, it was felt, was more likely to become a negative influence. Sapper, the General Secretary of the Association of Cinematograph, Television and Allied Technicians, stated the argument in the following terms during the 1986 TUC conference debate.

> We reject the proposition that the state should determine union laws. It divides the strength and unity of the movement [11].

But, for a majority, maybe partly encouraged by the political fund experience, ballots, including those concerned with strikes, were to form an acceptable part of the industrial relations landscape for the foreseeable future. The TUC General Secretary, Willis, affirmed the new belief:

> Balloting is here to stay, because our members favour it. We are committed to making the trade union movement even more representative and more democratic because that way we will be stronger and more effective [12].

If the 1984 Act was to be repealed, a procedure had to be designed to ensure that individual members could somehow enforce a ballot; it was at this juncture that the break with the traditional stance on union autonomy was made. Again, according to Willis:

> The new statutory framework will also entail general principles for inclusion in union rule books. These will be based on a right for union members to have a secret ballot on decisions relating to strikes, and for the method of election of union executives to be based on a system of secret ballots. But there will be no imposition of rigid procedures [13].

Whereas the 1984 Act made it difficult to use other than postal balloting, Willis is clearly anxious to extend the potential of workplace ballots:

> We want ballots - with proper facilities, polling stations at the workplace, meetings in working time [14].

This would seem a particularly sensible approach, especially bearing in mind the review ballots which produced a significantly higher turnout in workplace as against postal ballots.

The TUC-Labour Party document aims at enshrining the rights of individual union members, but differs fundamentally from the 1984 Act in one crucial respect. The 1984 legislation made the enjoyment of immunities dependent upon the conduct of a ballot; under the new proposals, immunities would exist regardless of whether a ballot had been held. Furthermore, the 1984 Act provided for ballots in relation to all industrial action in breach of the contract of employment. The TUC-Labour Party proposals concerned themselves only with strikes.

After defining what they regard as an effective right for unions' members, the TUC and the Labour Party are then logically required to provide a system of enforcement. The format agreed upon was an independent tribunal 'that will have the duty of acting on complaints by union members that the statutory principles have been breached. This will be presided over by a legally qualified person. The tribunal would adopt a conciliatory and flexible approach but would ultimately, after conducting an investigation, be empowered to require a union to take the necessary steps to remedy the complaint. In common with the procedures relating to other tribunals of this kind, appeal to the ordinary courts will only be permitted on a point of law' [15].

Perhaps a number of conclusions emerge from this discussion. Firstly, by accepting some form of statutory enforcement of ballots, trade unions appear to feel that it would be politically difficult, especially given the experience of the 1984/85 coal industry dispute, to argue for a framework in which there is no procedure to enforce ballots. Secondly, regardless of whatever language may be used, the unions have shown themselves prepared to tolerate a level of state involvement in their affairs, albeit dependent upon an extensive new provision of individual and collective rights, which they would earlier have felt compelled to reject. And, thirdly, despite the perceived political necessities, it could be that the experience of ballots, coupled with the campaigning opportunity which they offered, has been such as to minimise fears and to awaken expectation. It is ironic in this context that the political fund review ballots which did so much to establish confidence were not even mentioned in People at Work. The document discussed neither the balloting requirements nor the future ground rules for trade union political funds.

SUMMARY

The significance of the review ballots is to be found in the way in which that experience has influenced the debate on other issues. Directly, it is because of the review ballots that the question of political funding is likely to generate more interest than for some time, but, now in conditions where the trade unions do not need to be on the defensive. Also, it is because of the conclusions drawn from the review ballot campaign that it is recognised that a healthy link between the Labour Party and the trade unions depends upon finding means of ensuring greater involvement of trade unionists at local level in the Labour Party. In addition, because of the success of the review ballots, the whole process of balloting is now viewed with considerably less trepidation by trade unionists. This chapter has looked at these issued, and tried to emphasise means of possible development.

NOTES

1. Ewing in Lewis (1986, p. 305) draws attention to the interesting point that 'in Sweden and in the federal laws of Australia and Canada, trade unionists have no legally

enforceable right to claim exemption from the obligation to finance the political activities of their union'.

2.   The 1986 Annual Labour Party Conference decided to defer further consideration on this issue until after the forthcoming general election.

3.   The Advisory, Conciliation and Arbitration Services, Annual Report, 1985, p. 15.

4.   Rookes v Barnard (1964) AC 1129.

5.   TUC/Labour Party, 'People at Work: New Rights, New Responsibilities, p. 4.

6.   People at Work, p. 15.

7.   People at Work, p. 15.

8.   People at Work, p. 16.

9.   People at Work, p. 19.

10.   John Edmonds, General Secretary of GMBATU, as reported in The Times, 2nd September 1986.

11.   Alan Sapper, as reported in The Times, 2nd September, 1986.

12.   Normal Willis, TUC General Secretary, as reported in The Times, 2nd September, 1986.

13.   As reported in The Times, 2nd September, 1986.

14.   As reported in The Times, 2nd September, 1986.

15.   People at Work, p. 21.

CONCLUSION

At the time of writing, many political commentators are suggesting that a period of politics associated personally with the Prime Minister, Margaret Thatcher, and with a particular set of ideas or perspectives, is coming to an end. Political commentators have too often prematurely announced the demise of a particular politician, or policies, for it to be prudent to invest too heavily in their conclusions. However, if they are correct, it would be welcome news for the trade unions, as it should signal the end of those policies which have sought to reduce trade union power. A more moderate Conservative administration might be expected to seek out a degree of common ground, or understanding with the unions; a Labour Government would offer the prospect of the enactment of a positive charter of rights for trade unions, and for employees and a broader partnership over a range of issues. If this new political scenario eventually emerges, the question will remain as to the influence of the review ballots upon the recasting of British politics.

For the reasons already stated in earlier chapters, the Government must have held every expectation that most, if not all, unions would have rejected the continuation of political funds; and, that, as a result, the Labour Party would have been severely, if not fatally, wounded. The possibility of such an outcome must have been tempting in the extreme to many Conservatives and Government Ministers.

What happened in practice, of course, was the very opposite: trade unionists voted in large numbers to re-affirm the existence of political funds, and, hence, the unions' political role. With that result, the Government had provided the whole Labour movement with an unexpected bonus for the reasons which we have already developed:

(a) The review ballots represented a substantial and real victory for the trade unions at a time when victories were rare, if not extinct.

(b) The campaigns leading to the eventual results had shown an analysis and imagination unrivalled amongst trade unions for many years. The campaign had demonstrated that, through careful analysis of the viewpoints and aspirations of members, it was possible to develop a focus at the workplace which met those aspirations and built upon them. The platitude that labour movement campaigns are not won simply through packed meetings for the already committed was reinforced time and again, as individual unions held their own ballots.

(c) As a result of the success of the review ballots, and the new insights into campaigning, the trade unions, through TUFL, have felt sufficiently confident to organise a substantial programme aimed at persuading their members to support, to join, and to campaign for the Labour Party. If this programme only achieves some of the aspirations, it will, nevertheless, be in sharp contrast to the earlier years of depoliticisation to which reference was made in Chapter 3. Thanks to the actions of a Conservative Government, the unions have decided to adopt more of a political posture in their relationship with individual members.

(d) Because of the overwhelming support which was secured in the review ballots, the links between the Labour Party and the unions should benefit both negatively and positively: negatively, because the powerful case used by the Conservatives in which they contended that trade unionists wished to ascribe a non-political role to their union, is now severely weakened, if not killed off altogether; and, positively, because with the new confidence which has emerged, the unions can now pursue a new relationship with the Labour Party at both local and national levels.

(e) Ironically, it is now the institutional financing of the Conservative Party which, given that it is not supported by democratic decision, appears illegitimate and difficult to defend. Come the next election, it is the Conservative Party which will be on the defensive concerning their funding from companies; for that part of their income which they receive from trade unions, the Labour Party need seek no alternative legitimacy but the review ballot results.

Maybe all these implications flowing from the 1984 Act, and its implementation in relation to political funds, will not totally change the face of British politics. That would be too much to expect. What has happened, however, is that the 1984 Act has worked in a way which its architects never

CONCLUSION

expected and never wished for; for that, the labour movement can be both thankful, and self-congratulatory, as the period April 1985 - March 1986 will, no doubt, be recorded as one of the most successful chapters in the history of British trade unionism. Admittedly, success was on an agenda imposed by others; maybe, the review ballots will encourage the unions to seek success on their own agenda.

APPENDIX
REVIEW BALLOT RESULTS

A. Overall Statistics:

Total ballot papers issued	6,984,603	
Total ballot papers returned	3,561,321	(50.99%)
Total YES	2,957,235	(83.03%)
Total NO	656,534	(18.43%)
Majority of YES over NO	2,300,701	

B. Individual union results are set out below, showing number of papers issued, turnout and YES/NO votes. They are arranged in chronological order of balloting.

POLITICAL FUND BALLOTS: INDIVIDUAL UNION RESULTS

1. Society of Graphic & Allied Trades: 7th May 1985

Ballot papers issued	208,686	
Returned	118,563	(56.8% turnout)
YES	91,760	(78% YES)
NO	25,947	(21% NO)
Spoilt/Blank	856	
MAJORITY	65,813	

2. Iron and Steel Trades Confederation: 23rd May 1985

Ballot papers issued	48,859	
Returned	33,037	(67.7% turnout)
YES	28,633	(86.7% YES)
NO	4,404	(13.3% NO)
Spoilt	93	
MAJORITY	24,229	

121

APPENDIX

3. Furniture, Timber and Allied Trades: 3rd June 1985

Ballot papers issued	80,194	
Membership declared to		
Certification Officer	54,300	
Returned	15,791	(30% turnout)
YES	11,410	(72% YES)
NO	4,269	(28% NO)
Spoilt	112	
MAJORITY	7,141	

4. Union of Communication Workers: 20th June 1985

Ballot papers issued	195,698	
Returned	135,883	(69.4% turnout)
YES	102,546	(75.5% YES)
NO	33,337	(24.5% NO)
MAJORITY	69,209	

5. National Communication Union: 28th June 1985

Ballot papers issued	121,037	
Returned	95,276	(78.7% turnout)
YES	77,183	(81% YES)
NO	17,757	(19% NO)
Spoilt	336	
MAJORITY	65,813	

6. General Municipal Boilermakers and Allied Trades Union: 8th July 1985

Ballot papers issued	824,726	
Returned	503,083	(61% turnout)
YES	448,426	(89% YES)
NO	54,637	(11% NO)
MAJORITY	393,769	

7. Association of Professional, Clerical and Executive Staffs: 22nd July 1985

Ballot papers issued	90,132	
Returned	53,989	(59.9% turnout)
YES	39,465	(73.01% YES)
NO	14,380	(26.64% NO)
Spoilt	144	
MAJORITY	24,941	

8. Bakers, Food, and Allied Workers Union: 29th July 1985

Ballot papers issued	35,859	
Returned	22,246	(62.04% turnout)
YES	19,954	(89.70% YES)
NO	2,237	(10.06% NO)
Spoilt	55	
MAJORITY	17,662	

9. Amalgamated Union of Engineering Workers (Engineering Section): 6th August 1985

Ballot papers issued	808,800	
Returned	283,003	(37% turnout)
YES	238,604	(84% YES)
NO	44,399	(16% NO)
MAJORITY	194,205	

10. Electrical, Electronic, Telecommunications and Plumbing Union: 13th August 1985

Ballot papers issued	362,047	
Returned	167,743	(45% turnout)
YES	140,913	(84% YES)
NO	26,830	(16% NO)
MAJORITY	114,083	

11. National Union of Railwaymen: 23rd August 1985

Ballot papers issued	135,293	
Returned	82,667	(61.1% turnout)
YES	71,907	(87.2% YES)
NO	10,580	(12.8% NO)
MAJORITY	61, 327	

12. Power Loom, Carpet Weavers and Textile Workers Union: 23rd August 1985

Ballot papers issued	3,350	
Returned	2,976	(88.7% turnout)
YES	2,242	(75.3% YES)
NO	697	(24.7% NO)
MAJORITY	1,545	

APPENDIX

13. Associated Society of Locomotive Engineers and Firemen:
1st September 1985

Ballot papers issued	24,211	
Returned	20,672	(85.4% turnout)
YES	19,110	(92.4% YES)
NO	1,491	(7.2% NO)
Spoilt	71	
MAJORITY	17,629	

14. Transport Salaried Staff Association: 3rd September 1985

Ballot papers issued	49,324	
Returned	33,132	(67.2% turnout)
YES	22,975	(69.3% YES)
NO	10,017	(30.2% NO)
Spoilt	140	
MAJORITY	12,958	

15. National Union of Seamen: 3rd September 1985

Ballot papers issued	21,040	
Returned	7,142	(34% turnout)
YES	6,179	(86.5% YES)
NO	963	(13.5% NO)
Spoilt	364	
MAJORITY	5,216	

16. Ceramic and Allied Trades Union: 13th September 1985

Ballot papers issued	32,124	
Returned	23,602	(73.4% turnout)
YES	17,967	(76.12% YES)
NO	5,383	(22.8% NO)
Spoilt	252	
MAJORITY	12,694	

17. National Union of Scalemakers: 7th October 1985

```
Ballot papers issued      1,095
Returned                    595    (54% turnout)
YES                         460    (77% YES)
NO                          135    (23% NO)
Spoilt                        1

MAJORITY                    325
```

18. Transport and General Workers Union: 15th October 1985

```
Ballot papers issued    1,307,873
Returned                  647,113    (49.5% turnout)
YES                       511,014    (78.9% YES)
NO                        119,823    (18.2% NO)
Spoilt                     16,276

MAJORITY                  391,191
```

19. Confederation of Health Service Employees: 25th October 1985

```
Ballot papers issued      220,000
Returned                   88,743    (40.3% turnout)
YES                        81,012    (91.3% YES)
NO                          7,731    (8.7% NO)

MAJORITY                   73,281
```

20. National Union of Domestic Appliance and General Operatives: 30th October 1985

```
Ballot papers issued      4,196
Returned                  2,841    (67.71% turnout)
YES                       2,388    (84.47% YES)
NO                          439    (15.53% NO)
Spoilt                       14

MAJORITY                  1,939
```

APPENDIX

21. National Union of Tailor and Garment Workers: 30th
    October 1985

Ballot papers issued	66,400	
Returned	58,033	(87.4% turnout)
YES	52,634	(90.7% YES)
NO	4,968	(8.6% NO)
Spoilt	431	
MAJORITY	47,666	

22. National League for Blind and Deaf: 30th October 1985

Ballot papers issued	2,978	
Returned	2,458	(82.54% turnout)
YES	2,218	(90.21% YES)
NO	221	(9.8% NO)
MAJORITY	1,997	

23. National Union of Footwear, Leather and Allied Trades:
    3rd December 1985

Ballot papers issued	32,276	
Returned	27,232	(84% turnout)
YES	20,956	(77% YES)
NO	5,963	(22% NO)
Spoilt	313	
MAJORITY	14,993	

24. Union of Shop, Distributive and Allied Workers: 9th
    December 1985

Ballot papers issued	387,795	
Returned	152,976	(39.5% turnout)
YES	134,592	(88% YES)
NO	17,824	(11% NO)
Spoilt	560	
MAJORITY	116,768	

25. Association of Cinematograph, Television and Allied
    Technicians: 12th December 1985

Ballot papers issued	24,900	
Returned	12,192	(49% turnout)
YES	7,149	(59% YES)
NO	5,043	(41% NO)
MAJORITY	2,106	

26. National Graphical Association: 16th December 1985

Ballot papers issued	121,686	
Returned	87,693	(72.6% turnout)
YES	68,559	(78.2% YES)
NO	18,931	(21.6% NO)
MAJORITY	49,628	

27. Tobacco Workers Union: 17th December 1985

Ballot papers issued	11,438	
Returned	8,711	(76% turnout)
YES	7,790	(89.6% YES)
NO	905	(10% NO)
Spoilt	16	
MAJORITY	6,885	

28. National Association of Colliery Overmen, Deputies and
    Shotfirers: 13th January 1986

Ballot papers issued	15,000	
Returned	11,428	(76.19% turnout)
YES	9,930	(87% YES)
NO	1,481	(13% NO)
Spoilt	17	
MAJORITY	8,459	

APPENDIX

29. Technical Administrative and Supervisory Section
    (TASS): 15th January 1986

Ballot papers issued	219,885	
Returned	120,937	(55% turnout)
YES	91,389	(76% YES)
NO	29,467	(24% NO)
Spoilt	81	
MAJORITY	61,922	

30. National Union of Public Employees: 23rd January 1986

Ballot papers issued	660,863	
Returned	391,602	(59.3% turnout)
YES	329,442	(84.1% YES)
NO	60,332	(15.4% NO)
Spoilt	1,828	
MAJORITY	269,110	

31. Rossendale Union of Boot, Shoe and Slipper Operatives:
    3rd February 1986

Ballot papers issued	3,812	
Returned	1,605	(40% turnout)
YES	1,244	(77.5% YES)
NO	358	(22% NO)
Spoilt	3	
MAJORITY	886	

32. General Union of Associations of Loom Overlookers: 10th
    February 1986

Ballot papers issued	1,202	
Returned	1,109	(92.4% turnout)
YES	928	(83.5% YES)
NO	176	(16.02% NO)
Spoilt	5	
MAJORITY	752	

APPENDIX

33. Musicians Union: 3rd March 1986

Ballot papers issued	37,600	
Returned	13,745	(36.5% turnout)
YES	10,492	(76.33% YES)
NO	3,237	(23.55% NO)
Spoilt	16	
MAJORITY	7,255	

34. National Union of Mineworkers: 13th March 1986

Ballot papers issued	140,276	
Returned	106,610	(76% turnout)
YES	96,226	(90.25% YES)
NO	9,958	(9.34% NO)
Spoilt	426	
MAJORITY	86,268	

35. Fire Brigades Union: 17th March 1986

Ballot papers issued	43,948	
Returned	38,424	(87.4% turnout)
YES	30,607	(79.6% YES)
NO	7,652	(11.4% NO)
MAJORITY	22,955	

36. Association of Scientific Technical and Managerial Staff: 21st March 1986

Ballot papers issued	
Returned	126,441
YES	102,334
NO	23,996
MAJORITY	78,338

37. Union of Construction Allied Trades and Technicians:
     24th March 1986

     Ballot papers issued   250,000
     Returned   62,028   (25% turnout)
     YES   56,733   (91.5% YES)
     NO   5,295   (8.5% NO)

     MAJORITY   51,438

In addition, the Scottish Carpet Workers Union, which was
affiliated only to the Scottish TUC and which was not part of
TUCC also was required to hold a ballot. Their result was as
follows:

     YES Vote   664   - (88%)
     NO Vote   93   - (12%)

SELECTED BIBLIOGRAPHY

Allen, V. (1966) Militant Trade Unionism, Merlin Press, London

Banks, J. (1974) Trade Unionism, Collier-MacMillan, London

Barratt-Brown, M. (1972) From Labourism to Socialism, Spokesman Books, Nottingham

Clarke, T. and Clements, L. (1977) Trade Unions Under Capitalism, Fontana, London

Clarke, R.O., Fatchett, D.J. and Roberts, B.C. (1972) Workers Participation in Management in Britain, Heinemann, London

Cliff, T. (1975) The Crisis: Social Contract or Socialism, Pluto Press, London

Coates, D. (1975) The Labour Party and The Struggle for Socialism, Cambridge University Press, Cambridge

Coates, K. and Topham, A. (1972) The New Unionism, Peter Owen, London

Coates, K. and Topham, A. (1986) Trade Unions and Politics, Basil Blackwell, Oxford

Crouch, C. (1979) The Politics of Industrial Relations, Fontana, London

Ewing, K.D. (December 1984) 'Trade Union Political Funds: The 1913 Act Revised', Industrial Law Journal

Fatchett, D.J. (Autumn 1984) 'Trade Union Political Funds', Industrial Relations Journal, Vol. 15, No. 3

Fatchett, D.J. and Ogden, S. (April 1984) 'Public Expenditure Cuts and Job Loss: A Union Response', Journal of Management Studies, Vol. 21, No. 2

Fryer, R.H. (1979) 'British Trade Unions and the Cuts', Capital and Class, Vol. 8

Goldthorpe, J.H., Lockwood, D., Bechhofer, F. and Platt, J. (1968) The Affluent Worker: Industrial Attitudes and Behaviour, Cambridge University Press, Cambridge

Gramsci, A. (1955, reprinted) 'Sindicalismo e Consigli' in L'Ordine Nuovo, 1919-20, p. 45

Hain, P. (November 1984) 'An Unhappy Marriage? The Labour-Union Link', Marxism Today

BIBLIOGRAPHY

Hyman, R. and Brough, I. (1975) Social Values and Industrial Relations, Basil Blackwell, Oxford

Leopold, J. (Winter 1986) 'Trade Union Political Funds: A Retrospective Analysis', Industrial Relations Journal, Vol. 17, No. 4

Lewis, R. (1986) Labour Law in Britain, Basil Blackwell, Oxford

Marsh, A. and Coker, E. (1963) 'Shop Steward Organisation in the Engineering Industry', British Journal of Industrial Relations, Vol. 1, No. 1

McCarthy, W.E.J. and Parker, S. (1986) Shop Stewards and Workshop Relations, HMSO, London

Middlemass, K. (1979) Politics in Industrial Society: the Experience of the British System since 1911, London, Deutsch

Minkin, L. (1980) The Labour Party Conference, Manchester University Press

Minkin, L. (5th October 1977) 'The Labour Party has not been Hijacked', New Society

Pimlott, B. and Cook, C. (1982) Trade Unions in British Politics, Longman, Harlow

Pinto-Duschinsky, M. (1981) British Political Finance, 1830-1980, American Enterprise Institute for Public Policy Research, London

Royal Commission on Trade Unions and Employers Associations 1965-68 (June 1981) Report, HMSO, London, Cmnd 3623

Richter, I. (1973) Political Purpose in Trade Unions, Allen and Unwin, London

Saville, J. (1957-8) 'The Welfare State', New Reasoner, No. 3

Taylor, R. (1980) The Fifth Estate, Britain's Unions in the Modern World, Pan, London

Turner, H.A. (1962) Trade Union Growth, Structure and Policy, Allen and Unwin, London

Undy, R. and Martin, R. (1984) Ballots and Trade Union Democracy, Basil Blackwell, Oxford

Webb, B. (1956) Diaries 1924-32, ed. by Margaret Cole, Longman, London

INDEX

For Product Safety Concerns and Information please contact our EU
representative GPSR@taylorandfrancis.com
Taylor & Francis Verlag GmbH, Kaufingerstraße 24, 80331 München, Germany